Adapting to Climate Change

Claudia Morsut
Editor

Adapting to Climate Change

Implications of Risk-Based Approaches

palgrave
macmillan

Editor
Claudia Morsut
University of Stavanger
Stavanger, Norway

ISBN 978-3-032-07135-4 ISBN 978-3-032-07136-1 (eBook)
https://doi.org/10.1007/978-3-032-07136-1

This Palgrave Macmillan imprint is published by the registered company Springer Nature Switzerland AG.
The registered company address is: Gewerbestrasse 11, 6330 Cham, Switzerland

Preface

This book is about the implications of risk-based approaches to climate change adaptation and serves as the final result of the Research Council of Norway-supported project *RISKSEC2.0 Local Climate Change Adaptation: from Risk Governance to Securitisation Strategies*? that ran from October 2020 to March 2025. The project investigated how climate change adaptation policies and practices manifest in a multi-level governance context.

Throughout the years of the project, the research team looked for signs of securitisation of climate change adaptation at the international, national, and local levels, following the assumption that adaptation, as a policy response to climate change, followed the same path of the securitisation of climate change. However, the project results challenged and corrected this assumption, demonstrating the prominence of risk-based approaches to climate change adaptation both in national and local policies and practices, mainly at the municipality level. More specifically, adaptation is treated as a response to climate risks, using risk and vulnerability analyses and measures typical of risk management.

This book collects the final reflections related to risk-based approaches in adaptation, questioning the use of a risk management approach at the international, national, and local levels, the latter of which focus on Norway.

I hope you enjoy reading as much as I enjoyed managing and conducting research for this project, and I invite you to further explore the implications and consequences of risk approaches in adaptation.

Stavanger, Norway
June 2025

Claudia Morsut

Acknowledgements

This book was supported by the Research Council of Norway grant #302599.

The editor thanks the members of the research team willing to pursue this work beyond the end of the project period and contribute to the book's chapters, including the colleagues Elisabeth Angell, Ole Andreas Engen, Bjørn Ivar Kruke, Simon Neby from Norway, and Mark Rhinard from Stockholm University, who has been terrific with support and suggestions. Additional gratitude is extended to the three researchers who were not part of the project but were invited to contribute to this book thanks to their expertise in systemic risk governance.

Contents

Notes on Contributors

Elisabeth Angell is a societal economist and senior researcher at the Norwegian Research Centre (NORCE) in Bergen, Norway. She is interested in climate and environmental politics, Indigenous politics, regional politics, and development. She has extensive knowledge of Norwegian rural and regional politics and High North politics.

Paul Einhäupl is a researcher at RIFS, the Research Institute for Sustainability, Helmholtz Centre for Geosciences, Potsdam, Germany. His research explores how systemic risks emerge from the interactions between societal, technological, economic, and environmental systems. Drawing on expertise in system dynamics and stakeholder assessment, he analyses cross-sectoral interdependencies to address the complex governance challenges posed by systemic risks.

Ole Andreas Engen is a professor of Risk Management and Societal Security in the Department of Safety, Economics and Planning at the University of Stavanger, Stavanger, Norway. He holds a master's degree in Economics from the University of Oslo (1991) and a PhD in Sociology from the University of Bergen (2002). His primary research interests are how risk, safety, and security evolve at the intersection between technology, regulation, and politics.

Benjamin Hofbauer is a postdoctoral fellow at RIFS, the Research Institute for Sustainability, Helmholtz Centre for Geosciences, Potsdam, Germany. He completed his PhD at the Delft University of Technology, the Netherlands, where he developed a framework for the ethical governance of solar climate engineering. He focuses on the integration of philosophical reflections into the governance of systemic risks, with special attention on how co-creative approaches can be supplemented through ethical thinking.

Bjørn Ivar Kruke is a professor of Risk Management and Societal Security in the Department of Safety, Economics and Planning at the University of Stavanger, Stavanger, Norway. His main areas of study include crisis preparedness and response and learning after crises. His research is rooted in his own practical experience from crisis areas in the world and from training as a civil protection expert in the European Civil Protection Mechanism.

Claudia Morsut is an associate professor of Societal Security in the Department of Safety, Economics and Planning at the University of Stavanger, Stavanger, Norway. She holds a PhD in International Relations from the University la Sapienza, Rome, Italy. She studies the European Union's security governance, risk management and civil protection, climate change, and climate change adaptation in a multi-governance setting.

Simon Neby is a professor of Administration and Organisation Theory at the University of Bergen, Bergen, Norway, and is affiliated with the Centre for Climate and Energy Transformation. His research interests revolve around public organisations, politics, and governance in different sectors, typically focusing on institutional change, reforms, accountability, application of knowledge, coordination, capacity, and legitimacy, in addition to climate policy and climate transformations, across the distinction between mitigation and adaptation.

Mark Rhinard is a professor of International Relations at Stockholm University, Stockholm, Sweden, and the research director of the Swedish Institute of International Affairs. He earned his MPhil and PhD degrees from Cambridge University and taught at Oxford University before being awarded a postdoctoral position at Leiden University. His research interests include the institutional contexts of international cooperation, particularly as they apply to transboundary security threats, including terrorism, natural disasters, and pandemics.

Pia-Johanna Schweizer leads the Research Group Systemic Risk at RIFS, the Research Institute for Sustainability, Helmholtz Centre for Geosciences, Potsdam, Germany. She received an MA in Sociology and English/American Studies and a PhD in Sociology from Stuttgart University, Germany. She studies systemic risk, risk governance, and deliberative decision-making under risk and uncertainty. She is also interested in decision-making support efforts for risk management, as well as improving dialogue and cooperation of actors at all governance levels.

CHAPTER 1

The Relevance of Risk-Based Approaches in Climate Change Adaptation

Claudia Morsut

Abstract Climate change adaptation has become an important component of climate change governance. One approach that seems to have accompanied its rise on the international agenda is risk management. This introduction presents our understanding of adaptation and risk management. It summarises the findings from the RISKSEC2.0 project that ground the studies included in this book and outlines the challenge we aim to address, namely, the theoretical and empirical implications of using risk management in climate change adaptation to tackle the climate change challenge.

Keywords Climate change • Climate change adaptation • Risk Governance • Risk management • RISKSEC2.0 • Security Studies

C. Morsut (✉)
University of Stavanger, Stavanger, Norway
e-mail: claudia.morsut@uis.no

C. Morsut (ed.), *Adapting to Climate Change*,
https://doi.org/10.1007/978-3-032-07136-1_1

1.1 Introduction

Despite growing climate change scepticism, climate change impacts are undeniable. Societies worldwide have witnessed an increase in extreme weather-related events such as fires, floods, and heatwaves. There is enough available scientific evidence showing climate change's environmental, economic, and social consequences. Environmentally, sea-level rise, coastal erosion, the reduction of ice, the rise of temperatures, and the acceleration of species extinction are well documented. Forecasts on economic and social impacts paint a bleak picture in terms of greater costs for emergency response teams, increased damage to built assets, food scarcity, decreased freshwater availability, growing risks of conflict, and higher numbers of climate migrants.

Climate change has become a relevant research topic in several academic disciplines, but there are two that are the focus of this book: Security Studies and Risk Governance. In these two disciplines, research on climate change has grown significantly in recent decades. As the impacts of climate change increasingly intersect with global and national security concerns, Security Studies scholars have written extensively about climate change as a threat multiplier, exacerbating existing vulnerabilities such as resource scarcity and regional socio-economic fragilities (see Dalby, 2013; Floyd, 2015; McDonald, 2013; Trombetta, 2014). Several scholars have studied climate change through a securitisation theory lens, assuming that urgent measures need to be taken (see Albert, 2022; Diez et al., 2016; von Lucke, 2020) or exposing the challenges of securitising climate change (see Oels, 2012; Trombetta, 2019; Warner & Boas, 2020).

Risk Governance theorists have analysed climate risks—risks associated with climate change—at length. To cope with them, both adaptation and mitigation are necessary. Measures taken in both these responses are characterised by high levels of complexity, uncertainty, and ambiguity, since climate risks encompass both acute events and prolonged crises that cannot be resolved through simple or definitive solutions. In addition, Risk Governance researchers have promoted new concepts like systemic risks to better grasp the complexity climate change carries with it: climate risks are interconnected, and they provoke cascading effects across sectors, requiring risk-based approaches such as risk management, scenario planning, resilience-building, early warning systems, and multi-stakeholder collaboration (see Schweizer, 2021; Schweizer & Renn, 2019). This book follows this strand of research to conclude the

RISKSEC2.0 project, which took stock of the above relevant disciplines in its focus on climate change adaptation.

Climate change is not only a complex field of research, but it also poses considerable difficulties for public policy at all levels of governance. Internationally, the United Nations has boosted and supported an international climate regime, calling for strong responses to the climate crisis. In recent years, the European Union has taken a leading role in promoting a climate-resilient society by 2050 through its European Green Deal. Nationally, states develop policies and implement legislation and strategies to bring benefits to local levels of government, since they are the primary witnesses of climate change impacts. Indeed, if climate change is a global challenge that cannot be handled by a single actor, climate change consequences unfold locally with direct impacts on local communities.

The global community has adopted two main responses to fight climate change: mitigation and adaptation. This book delves into the latter, defining climate change adaptation as the varied and complex set of strategies, practices, and measures aiming at 'reducing climate risks through processes of adjustment in our ecological, social, or economic systems' (IPCC, 2023, p. 7). Since the 2015 Paris Agreement, adaptation has gained political momentum, reaching equal footing with mitigation, which consists of measures to reduce or cut greenhouse gases. Now included in several international, national, and local political agendas worldwide, spanning from the United Nations to local communities, adaptation has become the new mantra for building resilient societies able to cope with climate change.

Despite the Intergovernmental Panel on Climate Change's (IPCC) latest definition, however, climate change adaptation is not easy to identify. Similar to climate change, adaptation has been investigated by several disciplines—human geography, ecology, urban planning, development studies, political science, and international relations—and each discipline has contributed with insights into the scientific and practical understanding of adaptation based on the peculiarities of the discipline. There exist some common traits in these fields, particularly the classification of adaptation as social or economic change needed to reduce climate change impacts. At the same time, there are also substantial differences, since adaptation can be interpreted as an outcome, a process, or a means to reach more sustainable and resilient societies.

Furthermore, climate change adaptation involves a wide and varied range of public and private actors, ranging from local communities to governments, from NGOs to international organisations, that can propose different, if not contrasting, agendas. Adaptation measures can be of several types, from nature-based solutions to more sophisticated interventions via technological tools. Adaptation can occur in an anticipatory or proactive fashion through measures taken before climate change impacts manifest, like requiring flood insurance for private households independently from the probability of floods; adaptation can also be reactive and respond to a climate change impact that has occurred, like prohibiting rebuilding after a flood. When incorporated into public policy, adaptation can blend with preparedness, crisis management, risk management, urban planning, or sustainable development. In essence, climate change adaptation aims to develop solutions that integrate preparedness, planning, technology, and nature. Policymakers worldwide thus struggle with the diversity of actors and tasks involved in adapting to climate change and have adopted different approaches for conceptualising, understanding, and acting on the issue.

This book is interested in one approach that seems to have accompanied the rise of adaptation in the international agenda, namely, *risk management*. Generally, risk management is the systematic process of identifying, assessing, prioritising, and responding to potential risks. It involves evaluating the likelihood and impact of risks and implementing measures to mitigate them to enhance resilience. This definition is flexible and broad enough to be applied across fields, including climate change adaptation governance, and emphasises the strategic dimension of managing uncertainty. In some government arenas, risk management is a long-standing administrative practice, while in others it has been newly adopted to inform adaptation strategies and practices. This book shows how authorities address adaptation and capture its meaning through a risk management approach towards extreme weather events, sea-level rise, and long-term environmental shifts to reduce vulnerability, enhance resilience, and support sustainable development. In this definition, scientific knowledge, stakeholder cooperation, and policy outcomes aim to govern the uncertainty generated by climate risks through adaptation policies and measures.

The studies in this book also problematise the rise of a risk management approach to addressing climate change adaptation at various levels of government, since risk management is considered a type of policy logic that shapes and refracts the outcomes of the policymaking processes to which it is applied. Policy logics are underpinned by a set of ontological understandings of the nature of problems and how they should be handled, along with certain methodologies for analysing and acting upon those problems. Policy logics, in other words, are not politically neutral. As such, a risk management approach offers systematised models for making assessments and a clear set of decision tools. It also, however, may underestimate complexity, exclude wider social goals, trigger new unknown risks, or exacerbate insecurities.

1.2 The RISKSEC2.0 Project

The prominent role that climate change adaptation has gained in the international agenda was explored in the project *RISKSEC2.0 Local Climate Change Adaptation: from Risk Governance to Securitisation Strategies?* This project investigated adaptation policies, initiatives, and plans at the international, national, and local levels to better understand policy dynamics of adaptation in a multi-level governance setting and to what extent these policy dynamics influence each other. As several of these policies are top-down (see the Paris Agreement or the UN Development Goals), the project began with an investigation on adaptation, considering how international organisations like the United Nations and the European Union approach climate change adaptation. Then, the project expanded to the national and local levels, represented by the countries in the project's consortium (Norway, Sweden, and the Netherlands) and by four municipalities (two in Norway, one in Sweden, and one in the Netherlands).

The exploration of adaptation relied on securitisation theory and the literature on the securitisation of climate change which allowed to understand how different levels of governance frame adaptation and what this means in terms of opportunities for complementary efforts between international, national, and local climate change adaptation programmes, pinpointing positive (shared understandings and coherent action) and negative (conflicting perspectives and local disempowerment) dynamics. The Risk Governance literature was a useful conceptual toolbox to understand to what extent climate change adaptation is embedded in a risk-based approach, especially at the local level.

Securitisation theory, in its classic academic formulation, describes the process by which elites transform issues into matters of security by labelling them as existential threats that require extraordinary responses (Buzan et al., 1998). It is an extreme form of politicisation—one that legitimises specific arguments, practices, and methods to be used in the name of security. The classic approach was relatively narrow, requiring extraordinary 'existential' speech acts that we rarely see today. Theoretical developments (see Balzacq, 2005; Bigo, 2002; Ciută, 2009) posit that securitisation may take place even without using security language and is more subtle but equally consequential.

One subtler version of securitisation is reflected in the literature on riskification. Riskification is more relevant today, some authors argue (Corry, 2012; Friis & Reichborn-Kjennerud, 2016), since it reflects the more everyday—even mundane—turns of phrase and guiding mindsets that shift policy outcomes. Rather than the utterance of an existential threat, riskification frames issues more broadly towards possible and random sources of harm that must be addressed. It assigns probabilities to known dangers and includes the mindset of bringing hazards 'under control' (often through technocratic processes). This view is consistent with a risk governance approach, which is the purposeful steering of behaviour towards the goals of analysing, understanding, and acting upon certain risks (IRGC, 2017; Olsen et al., 2019; van Asselt & Renn, 2011), promoting long-term precautionary governance.

Debate has erupted over whether riskification is a separate phenomenon from securitisation (Corry, 2012) or whether it exists on the same spectrum (Diez et al., 2016). The project sided with the latter but still took great interest in whether traditional securitisation (that the project indicated as threatification) was the dominant dynamic in climate change adaptation governance. The project, indeed, started with the assumption that since there are signs of securitisation of climate change at the international and national levels, securitisation processes may have shaped adaptation policies as well. This assumption was explored in relation to its practical consequences for the local level, since securitisation can affect decision-making on climate change adaptation at higher levels and may lead to transformational changes in local communities, which are not necessarily the most suitable for them.

Following the material turn, the project operationalised securitisation into three analytical categories beyond the classical speech acts to include discourses, actors, and tools. Discourses concerned words, concepts, narratives, and scripts used to describe climate change and climate change adaptation. The project investigated whether discourses reflected security sensibilities, who and what was presumed to be 'threatened' or 'at risk', and what was at stake. Actors were those legitimised by discourses to pursue adaptation policies, so the project focused on policymakers and civil servants working in the public administration. Tools serve as a broad category, including strategies, resources, and more practical means, such as technologies.

1.3 Insights from the RISKSEC2.0 Project

The novelty of the project was twofold: first, the shift of focus from the securitisation of climate change, a well-documented field of research especially at the national and international levels (see Barnett, 2003; Davoudi, 2014; McDonald, 2013; Von Lucke et al., 2014), to the securitisation of climate change adaptation, as policy response to climate change. The research team searched for pathways of adaptation from the international to the local level—including heightened political attention on adaptation, more focused adaptation responses to climate change, innovative solutions, the inclusion of new actors, and budget rearrangements—to detect signs of securitisation. Second, the assumption that securitisation is a process that happens not only at the international and national level, but also at the local level, thus led the research team to look for processes of securitisation in four municipalities, where it was assumed they would trickle down from the international level, almost according to a linear process. The research team hypothesised that it would find unnecessary extraordinary measures at the local level, the improper mobilisation of local resources, a lack of a proper understanding of local contextual factors, and worsening climate change impacts due to the pressure exercised by international policies on adaptation and the urgency to act.

The findings of the project constitute the backbone of this book. One finding pointed out that at the international level, climate change adaptation bears some signs of securitisation (Morsut & Rhinard, 2025). However, at the local level, the project's findings reveal that climate change adaptation has mainly been handled through a risk-based approach (Barquet et al., 2024; Jochemsen & Mees, 2024; Morsut et al., 2024) that has *normalised* the threat of climate change. In other words, where previous studies identify hints of securitisation of climate change internationally, these trends have not followed the treatment of adaptation at the national (see Rhinard et al., 2024) and, most of all, at the local levels analysed in the project. Risk-based approaches are evident in the range of risk management practices that, at a local level (the four municipalities), represent long-standing administrative routines: risk and vulnerability analyses, contingency plans, and already established risk tools, such as early warning systems or sensors, contribute to adapting to a changing climate. These risk-based approaches are characterised by technocratic governance, which focuses on protection and preparedness measures in addition to typical risk management tools such as risk analyses. The findings of the project revealed certain challenges in treating climate change adaptation as *business as usual*: the dominance of this approach, especially at local level, could impede the emergence of innovative strategies needed to address the complex challenges related to adapting to a changing climate and could hinder public participation in the development of such policy and practice.

All these findings pointed towards one direction: the dominant policymaking logic that accompanies climate change adaptation is risk management, a long-standing approach to handling urgent policy problems that, evidence shows, has been quickly adopted by officials handling adaptation. As such, this has been the focus of this book: adaptation, being so much more local and diffuse, runs into existing risk management principles and practices and is refracted from there because adaptation represents a host of different kinds of actions that must be dealt with in an everyday fashion. However, risk management carries some implications: by studying the nature of risk management policymaking for adaptation, we critically question whether risk management is realistically a comprehensive response to adaptation or whether it only encourages incremental changes. In addition, although risk management and climate change adaptation seek to find solutions for challenges that are not easily solved, both are addressed by separate communities of policymakers, practitioners, and researchers who often use different epistemological assumptions to deal with similar issues.

1.4 Debates and Issues Touched Upon in This Book

This book takes a novel approach by using climate change adaptation as a *tool* for reflecting on what it means to treat adaptation through a risk management approach. To do so, it takes stock of climate change adaptation policies at different government levels and the accompanying, but largely unquestioned, use of a risk management approach. In this way, the book both increases our understanding of climate change adaptation, including how it is being conceptualised and addressed, and raises questions relevant to the risk management concept and its implications for public policy making.

The book, as much as the project, addresses the question of how to define climate change adaptation. Despite the official definitions, the RISKSEC2.0 group uncovered competing meanings, demonstrating that the person or organisation that defines adaptation is also the actor who controls the policy and practice of adaptation.

Theoretically, the book speaks to two streams of literature on the implications of a 'risk' approach to the governance of extreme events: Security Studies and Risk Governance. These two disciplines shaped the theoretical and analytical framework of the RISKSEC2.0 project. Each of these fields is mined for key insights into the advantages and drawbacks of risk management, and the book will contribute directly to debates within these fields. Analytically, we assess policies in the light of these advantages and drawbacks and discuss the resulting implications. Empirically, then, the book expands our understanding of which climate change adaptation policies are being adopted at the international and national levels to reduce climate risks.

While we have general knowledge of the normative problems associated with risk-based approaches in the pursuit of public policy solutions (see Ansell & Baur, 2018; Aradau & van Munster, 2007), we know much less about risk management per se and how it impacts climate change adaptation goals. A central question guides the contributions to the book: *What are the theoretical and empirical implications of using risk management in climate change adaptation to tackle the climate change challenge?* We offer readers a scientifically grounded but easily accessible entry point to the question of climate change adaptation policy, including its key features and scope, while also providing a clear line of analysis in exploring what it means that adaptation is largely dealt with using risk management.

Through the chapters of this book, we aim to make a threefold contribution:

1. To better understand the relevance of risk management in climate change adaptation;
2. To highlight the advantages and disadvantages of using a risk management approach to address climate change adaptation;
3. To propose changes to existing adaptation policies, mainly at the international and national levels of governance.

1.5 Book Outline

Since the goal of this book is to investigate the implications of a risk management approach in adaptation from both a theoretical and empirical viewpoint, it begins with two chapters focused on theoretical and conceptual issues. Chapter 2 interrogates the main theoretical perspectives used throughout the RISKSEC2.0 project, namely those provided by the Security Studies and Risk Governance disciplines, and discusses and contrasts the concept of risk based on its scholarly understanding in these two disciplines. Whereas Security Studies problematises the concept of security by introducing risk as a way to move beyond threat-based logics of securitisation, Risk Governance treats risk as a foundational and extensively developed concept for understanding how societies manage uncertainty. As such, Chap. 2 reviews the risk understandings stemming from two different epistemological communities, which are contrasted and discussed in terms of *interfaces*. Chapter 3 explores the relevance of understanding climate risks as systemic risks, drawing on insights from systems thinking. It investigates systemic risk governance and how challenges related to climate change and climate change adaptation affect it. The chapter concludes with a call for integrated, anticipatory, and ethically grounded approaches to support systemic risk governance.

The remaining chapters in the book are more empirical, seeking out risk management approaches and practices at different levels of governance, following the approach taken during the RISKSEC2.0 project—namely, international, national, and local. Chapter 4 traces how the UN and EU have developed and institutionalised risk management models for climate change adaptation, identifying six generations of models that move from scenario-based assessments to transformative governance, while also highlighting the political and normative tensions of risk-based approaches. Chapter 5 argues that Norwegian policymaking concerning adaptation fits with the risk management narrative, while simultaneously raising issues of legitimacy. Chapter 6 also concerns Norway, discussing flood risks at the local level and how municipalities approach adaptation in the interplay between prevention and preparedness. Chapter 7 concludes the book by summarising the main themes from the chapters, delineating theoretical and practical implications and suggesting further research.

References

Albert, M. (2022). Climate emergency and securitization politics: Towards a climate politics of the extraordinary. *Globalizations.* https://doi.org/10.1080/14747731.2022.2117501

Ansell, C., & Baur, P. (2018). Explaining trends in Risk Governance: How problem definitions underpin risk regimes. *Risk, Hazards & Crisis in Public Policy, 9*(4), 398–430.

Aradau, C., & Van Munster, R. (2007). Governing terrorism through risk: Taking precautions, (un)knowing the future. *European Journal of International Relations, 13*(1), 89–115.

Balzacq, T. (2005). The three faces of securitization: Political agency, audience and context. *European Journal of International Relations, 11*(2), 171–120.

Barnett, J. (2003). Security and climate change. *Global Environmental Change, 13*(1), 7–17.

Barquet, K., Englund, M., & Rhinard, M. (2024). Climate adaptation in multi-level governance systems: Security, risk, or normal politics? *Risk, Hazards & Crisis in Public Policy, 15*(4), 441–467.

Bigo, D. (2002). Security and immigration: Toward a critique of the governmentality of unease. *Alternatives: Global, Local, Political, 27*(1), 63–92.

Buzan B., Wæver, O., & De Wilde, J. (1998). *Security: A new framework for analysis.* Lynne Rienner.

Ciută, F. (2009). Security and the problem of context: A hermeneutical critique of securitization theory. *Review of International Studies, 35*(2), 301–326.

Corry, O. (2012). Securitisation and 'riskification': Second-order security and the politics of climate change. *Millennium: Journal of International Studies, 40*(2), 235–258. https://doi.org/10.1177/0305829811419444

Dalby, S. (2013). The geopolitics of climate change. *Political Geography, 37*, 38–47.

Davoudi, S. (2014). Climate change, securitisation of nature, and resilient urbanism. *Environment and Planning C: Politics and Space, 32*(2), 360–375.

Diez, T., von Lucke, F., & Wellmann, Z. (Eds.). (2016). *The securitisation of climate change.* Routledge.

Floyd, R. (2015). Global climate security governance: A case of institutional and ideational fragmentation. *Conflict, Security & Development, 15*(2), 119–146. https://doi.org/10.1080/14678802.2015.1034452

Friis, K., & Reichborn-Kjennerud, E. (2016). From cyber threats to cyber risks. In K. Friis & J. Ringsmose (Eds.). *Conflict in cyber space: Theoretical, strategic and legal perspectives* (pp. 27–44). Routledge.

IPCC Intergovernmental Panel on Climate Change. (2023). *Climate change 2022: Impacts, adaptation and vulnerability.* Contribution of Working Group II to the Sixth Assessment Report of the Intergovernmental Panel on Climate Change [H.-O. Pörtner, D. C. Roberts, M. Tignor, E. S. Poloczanska,

K. Mintenbeck, A. Alegría, M. Craig, S. Langsdorf, S. Löschke, V. Möller, A. Okem & B. Rama (Eds.)]. Cambridge University Press. https://doi.org/10.1017/9781009325844

IRGC International Risk Governance Council. (2017). *Introduction to the IRGC risk governance framework, revised version*. EPFL International Risk Governance Centre.

Jochemsen, N., & Mees, H. (2024). Securitization of local adaptation: Signs of riskification in a Dutch region. *Risk, Hazards & Crisis in Public Policy, 15*(4), 419–440.

McDonald, M. (2013). Discourses of climate security. *Political Geography, 33*, 42–51.

Morsut, C., Engen, O. A., Neby, S., & Angell, E. (2024). Translations of climate change consequences at the local level: Climate change adaptation in Bergen and Stavanger municipalities in Norway. *Risk, Hazards & Crisis in Public Policy, 15*(4), 468–490.

Morsut, C., & Rhinard, M. (2025). The collective securitization of climate change: Implications for adaptation policy in the European Union and United Nations. *Review of International Studies*, 1–26. https://doi.org/10.1017/S0260210525100867

Oels, A. (2012). From 'securitization of climate change' to 'climatization' of the security field: Comparing three theoretical perspectives. In H. Scheffran, H. Brauch & J. Schilling (Eds.), *Climate change, human security, and violent conflict* (pp. 185–206). Springer.

Olsen, O. E., Juhl, K., Lindøe, P. H., & Engen, O. A. (Eds.). (2019). *Standardization and Risk Governance: A multi-disciplinary approach*. Routledge.

Rhinard, M., et al. (2024). Understanding variation in national climate change adaptation: Securitization in focus. *Environment and Planning C, 42*(4), 676–696.

Schweizer, P.-J. (2021). Systemic risks – Concepts and challenges for Risk Governance. *Journal of Risk Research, 24*(1), 78–93. https://doi.org/10.1080/13669877.2019.1687574

Schweizer, P.-J., & Renn, O. (2019). Governance of systemic risks for disaster prevention and mitigation. *Disaster Prevention and Management, 28*(6), 862–874.

Trombetta, M. J. (2014). Linking climate-induced migration and security within the EU: Insights from the securitization debate. *Critical Studies on Security, 2*(2), 131–147. https://doi.org/10.1080/21624887.2014.923699

Trombetta, M. J. (2019). Securitization of climate change in China: Implications for global climate governance. *China Quarterly of International Strategic Studies, 5*(1), 97–116. https://doi.org/10.1142/S2377740019500076

van Asselt, M. B. A., & Renn, O. (2011). Risk governance. *Journal of Risk Research, 14*(4), 431–449.

von Lucke, F. (2020). *The securitisation of climate change and the governmentalisation of security*. Palgrave Macmillan.

von Lucke, F., Wellmann, Z., & Diez, T. (2014). What's at stake in securitising climate change? Towards a differentiated approach. *Geopolitics, 19*, 857–884.

Warner, J., & Boas, I. (2020). Securitization of climate change: How invoking global dangers for instrumental ends can backfire. *Environment and Planning C: Politics and Space, 37*(8), 1471–1488. https://doi.org/10.1177/2399654419834018

CHAPTER 2

Understanding Risk from Different Disciplines

Claudia Morsut and Ole Andreas Engen

Abstract Risk is a concept that has become widespread and used in several research fields within the social and hard sciences, mainly to address probabilities that something bad can happen, including adverse effects and uncertain outcomes. The goal of this introductory chapter is to deepen the understanding of risk from different theoretical perspectives and to contrast them by formulating key implications that will serve as the foundation for the subsequent chapters of this book. The chapter explores why it is essential to examine risk and risk thinking across two disciplines – Security Studies and Risk Governance – as these two scholarly fields were the point of reference for the theoretical and subsequent analytical framework of the RISKSEC2.0 project. We will illustrate key distinctions and potential overlaps between risk understandings from the two disciplines, as they emerge from separate epistemic communities. In addition, we will propose interfaces on risk from Security Studies and Risk Governance, while reflecting on their implications.

Keywords Risk • Risk Governance • Risk management • Risk practices • Security Studies • Security practices • Uncertainty

C. Morsut (✉) • O. A. Engen
University of Stavanger, Stavanger, Norway
e-mail: claudia.morsut@uis.no; ole.a.engen@uis.no

C. Morsut (ed.), *Adapting to Climate Change*,
https://doi.org/10.1007/978-3-032-07136-1_2

2.1 Introduction[1]

This chapter explores the relevance of debating the concept of risk across the two disciplines that the RISKSEC2.0 project relied upon for its theoretical and subsequent analytical framework: Security Studies and Risk Governance. The process of building the RISKSEC2.0 analytical framework allowed us to reach certain conclusions concerning the significance of integrating insights from both Security Studies and Risk Governance to study climate change adaptation and build more adaptive and anticipatory systems for managing uncertainty concerning climate change consequences. This chapter aims to highlight risk conceptualisations and practical implications of risk from these scientific fields, which stem from distinct epistemic communities, focusing on how these fields have developed their understanding of risk, its practices, a strategies and policies. Indeed, despite certain convergences, the two disciplines often hold competing or seemingly incompatible views on risk (Corry, 2012; Renn, 2008). By analysing the extent of different approaches towards risk between the two disciplines, the chapter establishes so-called risk interfaces between Security Studies and Risk Governance, offering insights into their theoretical and practical intersections.

Risk is the core subject of Risk Governance, one of the pillars of Risk Science, which encompasses a broad spectrum of knowledge on topics such as risk assessment, perception, management, communication, and governance (Aven, 2020; Aven & Thekdi, 2022) within the public and private sectors. Risk is viewed in terms of measurable uncertainties and participatory approaches to dealing with risk. While risk is integral to many security concerns, such as climate change, terrorist attacks, and cyber risks, Security Studies only began engaging with risk as a conceptual tool after the end of the Cold War to emphasise power dynamics and socially constructed risks. The post-Cold War period saw a broadening and deepening of the security concept, leading to the adoption of terms like hazards, vulnerability, and exposure. Consequently, risk has emerged as a key term in the security discourse (Petersen, 2016). This evolution has given rise to

[1]This chapter deepens issues touched in the paper by Morsut and Engen: "Interfacing risk logic, riskification, and risk governance: some research implications". *ESREL 2023 - Proceedings of the 33rd European Safety and Reliability Conference: The Future of Safety in the Reconnected World*, 3–7 September 2023, University of Southampton, United Kingdom. European Safety and Reliability Association. ISBN 978-981-18-8071-1. DOI: 10.3850/978-981-18-8071-1_P524-cd.

two distinct strands of research in Security Studies: one views risk as an extension or instance of security (Petersen, 2008) while the other treats risk and security as separate but interrelated phenomena (Corry, 2012). Moreover, the growing integration of risk into Security Studies has reshaped the approach of this discipline towards threats, as Aradau and Van Munster (2007, 2008) and Gad and Petersen (2011) have highlighted, by arguing that the concept of risk has transformed the way security threats are perceived and addressed.

To understand the complexity of the contemporary world, which seems to be spiralling out of control, we call for an interdisciplinary approach to risk, bridging Security Studies and Risk Governance. We highlight the necessity of scrutinising applied concepts and practices, such as the precautionary principle, risk analysis, and governance, regardless of disciplinary boundaries. By doing so, we aim to enlighten the theoretical and practical implications of risk thinking across these two critical fields by showing how Risk Governance has informed Security Studies. We point out that Risk Governance has played a more significant role in reshaping how security threats are conceptualised, shifting the emphasis from state-centric deterrence to the proactive and long-term management of diffuse and complex risks. In practical terms, this transition calls for societal changes in how to address future harms, moving from reactive measures to precaution, resilience, and preparedness. However, while this shift allows for more flexible and forward-looking approaches to threats, it also bears the danger of depoliticising security by embedding it within routine and administrative practices.

The chapter is organised as follows: we begin by examining the understanding of the risk concept in Security Studies and Risk Governance respectively, highlighting their distinct foundations. We then continue by proposing three interfaces to illustrate the need for interdisciplinary integration: understanding of risk, management of risk, and practices of risk. Finally, the conclusion advocates for collaboration between the two disciplines to address contemporary risks, enhance policymaking, and examine the societal and political factors shaping risk prioritisations.

2.2 Risk in Security Studies

Security Studies or International Security Studies is one of the central fields of the international relations (IR) discipline. This field was established in the United States between WWI and WWII thanks to the seminal book by the political scientist Philip Quincy Wright, *A Study of War*, published in 1942. Security in Security Studies was understood in an IR framework as freedom from (negative security) and freedom to (positive security) (see Huysmans, 2002; McSweeney, 1999) and was tied to the state, against which existential and external threats were directed mainly towards its territory and sovereignty by other states through military means. Since the late 1940s, Security Studies started to promote an understanding of security wider than the military one, but still anchored to national security. For instance, nuclear deterrence became subject to several studies during the Cold War period (for an account, see Michaels, 2024). Subsequently, scholars began to focus on a range of military and non-military threats and dangers directed against national security, analysing these through IR theories and frameworks (for an account, see Buzan & Hansen, 2009).

The widening of security flourished after the end of the Cold War, from the early 1990s onwards, when scholars began to explore security related to economics, environment, and society, also in a post-national context due to the changed geopolitical landscape. In addition, the end of the Cold War opened the introduction of new concepts to sustain this widening of the security concept. The most prominent became the concept of risk, which, some scholars argued, was better equipped to make the post-Cold War security context more understandable (see, e.g., Williams, 2008). Events like 9/11, the consequent war on terrorism, and threats provoked by climate change consequences contributed to making risk a common term among Security Studies scholars.

Alongside the introduction of the concept of risk, studies emerged that sought to explain the relationship between risk and security, both at a conceptual and practical level (see Kessler, 2010; Petersen, 2008, 2011, 2016). These studies emphasise the difference between security and risk, in terms of ontologies, which have practical consequences for how challenges are addressed: while threats to security concern the individual sphere of identity and agency, risk refers to the potential for harm or loss that can occur within a society or group that should respond by anticipating and mitigating potential negative events that could disrupt the safety, security, or well-being of a collective.

Two prominent scholars are recurrent among the authors working with ontological differences between security and risk. The first one is the sociologist Ulrik Beck and his concept of a risk society (Beck, 1992). According to Beck, technological and industrial developments in the 1990s brought positive and negative consequences to global societies. On the one side, the world witnessed economic growth. On the other side, the same developments generated previously unknown risks, characterised by intentional or unintentional effects. Beck argued that societies were 'moving from a world of enemies to one of dangers and risks' (Beck, 1999, p. 3), within which risks are socially constructed. Beck contended that our societies have moved away from the so-called first modernity, within which risks were manageable and calculable, to the so-called second modernity. Here, risks are uncontrollable, uncertain, incalculable, unavoidable, and challenging to monitor and manage due to human and technological transformations.

According to Beck, who was profoundly impacted by the Chernobyl disaster in 1986, this is particularly true for the environmental sector, where risks are increasingly uncertain. Risk is something that has not yet become real, and thus, anticipating and preventing risks means avoiding the transformation of a risk into a reality. Consequently, decision-making in the face of risks is difficult because it can only address uncertainties. In addition, knowledge—or better, non-knowledge—plays a relevant role when actors make decisions to face risks. Since risk is uncertain and relates to an unknown future, non-knowledge indicates that decisions are taken in a context ranging from unknown unknowns to limited knowns (Beck & Wehling, 2012). Despite scientific contributions, societies still struggle to possess enough knowledge to deal with risks, also because knowledge tends to produce new and unknown knowledge. In Beck's view, risk is an essential characteristic of societies, and decision-makers seek to control uncertainty by managing risks.

The second distinguished scholar is Michel Foucault and his reflections on *dispositif* and governmentality. The notion of *dispositif* or 'apparatus' is explained by Foucault as the 'heterogeneous ensemble consisting of discourses, institutions, architectural forms, regulatory decisions, laws, administrative measures, scientific statements, philosophical, moral and philanthropic propositions – in short, the said as much as the unsaid. Such are the elements of the apparatus. The apparatus itself is the system of relations that can be established between these elements' (Foucault, 1980, p. 194). This definition fits with ideas of risk as a result of discursive and non-discursive practices proposed by authors such as Aradau and Van Munster (2007, 2008). As such, risk is constructed through practices such as precautionary measures following the precautionary principle and statistical quantification.

Governmentality consists of the institutions, laws, and procedures used by the state to exercise its power and control over its population (Foucault, 1997). Governmentality encompasses more than government since it includes the relationships, practices, instruments, and processes used by government as neoliberal control mechanisms (Friis & Reichborn-Kjennerud, 2016). As such, risk becomes part of this governmentality toolbox to deal with threats and dangers (Friis & Reichborn-Kjennerud, 2016). Security scholars who draw upon Foucault consider risk as a tool and its uncertainty as manageable, measurable, and calculable (see Aradau & Van Munster, 2007, 2008; Dean, 1999; Rasmussen, 2006).

We borrow from Petersen (2011, p. 696), who summarises efficiently how security scholars have built on Beck and Foucalt: '…risk studies within Security Studies cling to the very generalised descriptions of current social developments and trends; description such as "risk society", "culture of fear" or "risk/security *dispositifs*", which tends to conceal a possibly much greater variety of conceptual understandings in the daily practices of security agents'. In addition, we side with Petersen's proposal to label those scholars inspired by Foucault as representatives of the so-called critical risk studies. These scholars consider risk as 'an academic and analytical alternative' (Petersen, 2011, p. 701), if not 'a counter-concept to security' (Petersen, 2011, p. 702), shifting focus from threats and states to include Risk Governance practices and technological tools that explore new empirical issues such as migration (Bigo, 2002), terrorism (Aradau & Van Munster, 2007), and airport security (Salter, 2008).

There is a second group of scholars, labelled by Petersen (2011) as 'global risk management', that argues for risk as 'a counter-concept to security' (Petersen, 2011, p. 702). This group, however, relies on Ulrich Beck's risk society and uses risk management and risk analysis as risk practices to study disasters and crises affecting states. These scholars use risk to emphasise its difference from threats. While risks are not related to specific events and are unforeseen, threats are specific, intentional, and quantifiable. In addition, they focus on the transformative power of using the concept of risk: from known to unknown futures, from measurable to non-measurable threats, and from security to risk. Despite different premises, both critical risk studies and global risk management propose to move the conceptual centre from security to risk. The main consequence of this shift is that 'practices of risk increasingly "overlap" with those of security' (Kirk, 2020, p. 266).

There is another author who deserves our attention, Olaf Corry (2012). Corry starts his argument about risk and security from another premise, namely the Copenhagen School's securitisation theory, one of the most prominent Security Studies theories developed in the 1990s. Securitisation theory poses that through speech acts and practices—the latter introduced during the so-called material turn of securitisation (Bengtsson et al., 2018; Bigo & Tsoukala, 2008)—securitising actors call for exceptional measures to protect and defend a referent object (e.g. states, ecosystems, societies) that is threatened by a referent subject. Securitisation theory emphasises the social construction of threats by securitising actors. To develop his critique towards the meaning of threats in securitisation theory, Corry applies the term risk to show that there is an ontological difference between risk and threat—as understood in securitisation theory—by introducing riskification and its underlying risk logic. According to Corry, a threat may be 'external and ungovernable' (Corry, 2012, p. 248) but, at the same time, the source of the threat is identifiable. As such, it is possible to intervene with urgent actions and measures.

On the other hand, risk concerns 'the possibility of harm' (Corry, 2012, p. 249), which means that the source of this harm is not known, identifiable, or clear. As such, this uncertainty does not allow risks to be addressed through direct actions, but rather with long-term societal engineering, resilience, preparedness, precautionary measures, and adaptation. Although Corry describes risk along the same lines as his colleagues from critical risk studies and global risk management, he seeks to push a slightly different agenda by treating risk and security as two distinct concepts, since risk provides a distinct logic of danger that cannot be captured by securitisation theory, and its construction must be explored separately, even if this diminishes securitisation's viability (Corry, 2012; Huysmans, 2011). Most significant among these latter claims is that of one of the Copenhagen School's founders, Ole Wæver (2011, p. 474), who made the split stark: '…securitization is securitization, and risk is risk'. According to Corry (2012), security constructions in the form of threat and risk represent distinct approaches to security policy with varying and evolving characteristics and implications.

Despite the differences, we argue that all the scholars mentioned above have a 'utilitarian' approach to risk in common. In other words, they consider risk a useful *descriptor* to grasp and better explain changing *security practices* in a world where states and borders do not have the same importance as during the Cold War. The introduction of a risk vocabulary in

Security Studies has, as such, opened up scholarly research that shows how important it is to use the risk concept to describe how to control and manage security concerns in a different geopolitical context—in other words, how security practices have changed. Williams, for instance, points out that 'risk management is a never-ending process – it is about living with insecurity, not providing security through deterrence of the threat from an outside actor, as was the case in the Cold War' (2008, p. 66). The use of risk management as a security practice is, according to Williams, '…about managing possible events in the future – these events, which have yet to occur, become the motive for action today' (Williams, 2008, p. 62). Corry also underlines that security practices include 'prevention, probabilities, possible future scenarios and managing diffuse risks rather than about deterring foes or defending against identifiable and acute threats' (Corry, 2012, p. 236).

Security practices from a risk perspective are more diffuse and heterogeneous, since they do not respect the dichotomy typical of defence and deterrence of normal versus exceptional. They follow the precautionary principle and contingency planning due to future possibilities of harm; they promote long-term governance and routine and bureaucratic procedures to control uncertainty (Corry, 2012, pp. 245, 247; Salter, 2008; Van Munster, 2005); they consist of risk analyses, calculation, and management (Bigo & Tsoukala, 2008). Aradau et al. (2008) are the scholars who advocate most often for describing security practices differently when applying the concept of risk in Security Studies. In referencing their work, we witness a shift from security practices to risk practices *in* security. However, the outpouring of risk practices in security has consequences for the way threats and security are understood (Aradau & Van Munster, 2007, 2008; Petersen, 2008; Rasmussen, 2006), since threats are rarely directed towards states as monolithic entities but have become transnational, including pollution, terrorism, and epidemics that transcend national borders and need to be addressed through risk practices. In addition, security policies are shaped differently, as Kessler (2010, p. 17) explains: 'Not the avoidance of threats or the deterrence of enemies but the management of risks constitutes the specific rationale, defines current operations and provides background for future development of technology and strategies'.

Another commonality among these scholars is the shared understanding of risk as uncertainty. However, none of these scholars have challenged the understanding of uncertainty from a security angle. The meaning of uncertainty used by Beck or Aradau and van Munster is not the same as that developed by Security Studies following the IR tradition. Despite being a contested concept (see Katzenstein & Seybert, 2018; Rathbun, 2007), we side with Kessler (2010) when he argues that the debate is more about different notions of uncertainty, probability, and contingency rather than the concept of risk itself. At the same time, these different notions should be contrasted with the security language employed in Security Studies due to their diffusion in the years following the end of the Cold War.

2.3 Risk in Risk Governance

The discipline of Risk Governance is firmly rooted in the domain of Risk Science and bridges the gap between a theoretical understanding of risk and its practical applications, as it studies and proposes deliberate and systematic efforts to guide behaviours and decisions towards the objective of analysing, understanding, and mitigating risks in ways that are sustainable, ethical, and aligned with collective goals. It highlights the importance of critical evaluation, deliberative communication, and intersubjective values in navigating the uncertainties of an increasingly complex and interconnected world. As outlined in the International Risk Governance Council (IRGC, 2017) and by scholars such as van Asselt and Renn (2011), Risk Governance extends beyond technical assessments, since it serves as a foundational knowledge base from which effective governance strategies are developed and implemented. In addition, it leverages the principle of communicative rationality, as articulated by Habermas (2018), to promote transparent and participatory decision-making processes by ensuring that diverse stakeholders can engage in meaningful dialogue, aligning technical expertise with societal values to develop adaptive and inclusive approaches and solutions.

Habermas (2018) emphasises rational communicative actions, where stakeholders engage in dialogue to achieve mutual understanding and consensus on addressing risks. Habermas also advocates for dialogue-driven governance, where rational argumentation and ethical considerations shape decisions. This approach involves creating open channels of discussion among scientists, policymakers, businesses, and the public to align risk management practices with shared goals and values. Risk governance is ultimately a deliberate effort to guide and manage risks through comprehensive analysis, inclusive communication, and coordinated actions. Scholars like Renn have contributed significantly to the field by emphasising the importance of understanding complexity, fostering collaboration, and ensuring that decision-making processes are transparent, rational, and inclusive (see Habermas, 2018).

Therefore, communication—serving as a bridge between scientific expertise and societal values—plays a central role in the Risk Governance discipline as much as the development of scientific knowledge. Indeed, strengthening knowledge regarding an unwanted event and its consequences reduces uncertainty (Aven, 2020). This knowledge is produced by providing the best possible methods to categorise, assess, and measure risks and to develop strategies and plans to cope with risks, while all relevant knowledge from various disciplines is welcome when seeking to provide solutions to complex risk problems. According to van Asselt and Renn (2011), knowledge transfer should be inclusive and meaningful for a vast number of actors: stakeholders, experts, policymakers, and the general public, since trust and social support are crucial for the responsible governing of uncertain, complex, and/or ambiguous risks.

According to Renn (2008), Risk Governance highlights the need for adaptive and inclusive approaches that address complexity and uncertainty. Governance frameworks must remain flexible to accommodate the evolving nature of risks while fostering transparency and participation to build trust among stakeholders. This viewpoint underpins the heavy controversy between Habermas and Foucault on their differing views of power and rationality, with Habermas advocating for communicative rationality as a pathway to consensus and legitimacy, while Foucault criticises such universal claims, emphasising power's pervasive and productive role in shaping knowledge and discourse. In the context of risk, governmentality highlights how risks are constructed, measured, and managed through frameworks that seek to regulate uncertainty and shape societal responses. Risk becomes a tool of governance, embedded in practices like surveillance, standard-setting, and risk communication, which aim to align individual and collective behaviours with broader political, economic, and social objectives. This perspective underscores how power operates not only through laws and institutions but also through subtle mechanisms that normalise certain risk perceptions and management strategies (Lupton, 2023).

There are several definitions of risk, but Risk Governance scholars generally follow a widely accepted definition, such as: '…an uncertain consequence of an event or activity with respect to something that humans value' (Aven, 2010, p. 626). While earlier definitions emphasised probability as a central concept, this definition focuses on uncertainty. As Aven and Krohn (2014, p. 1) argue, '...probability is just one tool for describing uncertainty, and the concept of risk should not be limited to this tool'. Uncertainty relates to the likelihood that an event will occur, the consequences of a potential event, and the severity of those consequences. Severity refers to the intensity, magnitude, extent, and scope of degradation to physical objects, social conditions, and values that people care about, such as homes, property, the environment, and human life. The concept of risk inherently pertains to the future, with probability and possibility relating to potential events (see Tierney, 2014).

The scholarly debate around this definition centres on whether it implies a realistic or constructivist understanding of risk. In the realistic perspective, '...risk exists independently of our perceptions and knowledge claims, subjective judgements, about what is at risk and how likely a risk will be realized' (Rosa, 1998, p. 32). Conversely, in the constructivist perspective, risk is viewed as a mental construct rather than an objective phenomenon. It results from our perceptions and interpretations, which shape how risks are evaluated (Renn, 2008).

Renn identifies four categories of risk based on their characteristics: simplicity, complexity, uncertainty, and ambiguity. A simple risk has a clear and widely accepted interpretation, with low uncertainty and evident negative consequences. In contrast, a complex risk makes it challenging to identify causal factors and establish cause–effect relationships, complicating the determination of which negative effects need to be addressed. Uncertain risks involve challenges related to limited or inadequate knowledge, making it difficult to calculate probabilities and potential consequences. Ambiguous risks, on the other hand, arise from differing understandings and interpretations of the same risk. These can be further classified into interpretative ambiguity, where evidence of risk is contested, and normative ambiguity, which concerns disagreements over values. Ambiguity introduces the need to address diverse legitimate viewpoints and balance trade-offs between various coping strategies. Risk Governance tackles ambiguity by fostering a common ground for characterising and qualifying both evidence and values to integrate multiple perspectives, enabling a more comprehensive and inclusive framework for managing the complexities of risk.

Risk Governance aligns with the traditions of regulatory sciences and policy analysis, focusing on the complex interplay of actors and organisations involved in risk-related decision-making processes (Bonholm and Corvellec, 2011; Renn, 2008; van Asselt & Renn, 2011). To enhance the efficiency of these processes, Risk Governance emphasises categorising risk problems, thereby avoiding the need to exhaustively explore all possible alternatives in every decision-making scenario (Aven, 2020; Renn, 2008). Evaluating whether an event is positive or negative—and to what extent—requires a foundation of shared values. These values are inherently intersubjective, gaining legitimacy through collective justification. For a value to be intersubjective, it must be well founded, which is particularly critical when addressing ambiguous risk problems. Ambiguity in Risk Governance arises in situations where 'several meaningful and legitimate interpretations of accepted risk assessment results' coexist (Renn, 2008, p. 77). Such ambiguity may stem from conflicting interpretations of risk problems or divergent normative judgements about them. Addressing ambiguous risk problems is most effective through deliberation. By employing communicative rationality, stakeholders can engage in discussions to reach consensus on values, priorities, and assumptions. This deliberative process mitigates ambiguity by fostering mutual understanding and aligning perspectives, ultimately enabling a more coherent and informed approach to Risk Governance (Aven, 2020; Renn, 2008).

Legitimacy is central to Risk Governance, as decisions with significant societal impact depend on trust and acceptance from diverse stakeholders. It is rooted in the perception that governance processes are fair, just, and necessary. As Foucault highlights, knowledge and expertise play a critical role in legitimising power, with scientific and technical experts often shaping the prioritisation and management of risks. However, legitimacy can be compromised when governance is perceived as undemocratic, opaque, or dominated by hidden agendas. Conflicts between economic interests and public health or safety, for instance, can erode public trust in governing institutions (Lupton, 2023).

2.4 Interfaces on Risk Between Security Studies and Risk Governance

By interfaces, we refer to *spaces* where two disciplines interact, creating opportunities for intersection and mutual influence that can benefit both. In regard to Security Studies and Risk Governance, we propose three interfaces: the understanding of risk, which entails the identification, framing, and interpretation of potential threats and opportunities across diverse contexts; the management of risk, encompassing the strategies, processes, and frameworks designed to mitigate, control, or capitalise on risks; and practices of risk, which involve actions, routines, and behaviours through which individuals and organisations navigate, internalise, and implement their approaches to risk. Together, these interfaces provide a framework for examining complexities within multifaceted environments.

2.4.1 *Risk Understanding in the Two Disciplines*

In Security Studies, risk is primarily understood as a social construct, shaped by where it is situated and contextualised and how it is perceived and understood. The socio-cultural context plays a pivotal role, reflecting the influence of societal, cultural, and political decisions and choices on how risks are framed. Constructivism, a theory of knowledge and learning, emphasises the active role of individuals in constructing their understanding of the world through experiences and interactions. Examined through the lens of constructivism, risk is shaped by human perceptions, cultural values, and contextual factors. Constructivism highlights the role of subjective interpretations, language, and power dynamics in defining and managing risks, underscoring that what constitutes a risk varies across societies and groups. Constructivism also recognises the influence of discourse in shaping collective understandings of risk, as well as the dynamic nature of risk, which evolves alongside new knowledge and circumstances.

In Risk Governance, there are scholars, such as Renn, who address risk similarly. However, the debate remains open on whether risk should be understood from a constructivist or realist perspective, as Rosa (1998) points out in his definition of risk. The constructivist understanding of risk in Risk Governance emphasises the importance of engaging diverse stakeholders, fostering dialogue and shared learning to address complex and emerging risks. While the realist critics suggest this approach may downplay measurable, objective aspects of risk, constructivism provides a holistic framework that integrates social, cultural, and relational dimensions, thereby enriching traditional approaches to risk management. If we look at the International Risk Governance Council (IRGC) Framework (2017), risks are predominantly understood through a realist lens, which acknowledges their tangible and measurable aspects, and a normative perspective, which considers how risks should be evaluated and managed in line with societal values, ethical standards, and policy objectives. When combined, this dual approach—risk as a construct and risk as objective—allows for a more pragmatic focus on mitigating risks' effects while aligning responses with broader governance principles and collective goals.

The key determinants of risk—uncertainty, contingency, pre-emption, and prevention—remain central in both Security Studies and Risk Governance. Uncertainty is a shared element in the risk understanding in both disciplines. However, Risk Governance approaches risk as uncertainty, tied to outcomes and consequences of decisions or events that may impact something of value. To cope with this uncertainty, Risk Governance relies on knowledge about likelihoods or outcomes, without necessarily focusing on identifying or addressing their root causes, as in Security Studies. The exception in Security Studies is Corry, who sides with an understanding of uncertainty in line with that of Risk Governance. In his attempt to distinguish threat from risk, Corry considers risk as addressing 'the possibility of harm' (Corry, 2012, p. 247), which means that the source of this harm is not known, identifiable, or clear. However, uncertainty implies a lack of knowledge, where probabilities are unclear or unknowable, as in 'unknown unknowns'.

In the understanding of risk, both disciplines consider time a variable that shapes how risk is understood and managed. Risk Governance is future-oriented about risk, using anticipatory tools like scenario planning and resilience strategies to cope with risks, emphasising long-term procedures and preparedness, based on the assumption that risks lie ahead, and we can be prepared for them. In Security Studies, time is often marked by urgency and exception. However, the outpouring of risk-related practices in security has transitioned from a security approach concerning immediate threats to a security approach addressing long-term vulnerabilities, implying a shift in strategies for coping with risk.

2.4.2 Risk Management in the Two Perspectives

Both Security Studies and Risk Governance emphasise risk management and decision making as the key domains where experts and policymakers collaborate or should collaborate to address risks. Risk management involves the process of identifying, assessing, and controlling risks, while decision-making is the process by which governments, organisations, or institutions develop and implement rules, regulations, and guidelines to address specific issues or achieve certain goals.

In both disciplines, there exist comparable categories of actors: those who govern and those who are governed. In Risk Governance, actors are risk managers, scientists, and policymakers dealing with specific risks to enhance societal resilience (Aven, 2020; Renn, 2008). Governments, public institutions, private agencies, and industry organisations are risk management actors as well, since they are legitimised to handle risks.

However, a major policy challenge for risk management and governance is to bring together local, national, and even supra-national actors, private as well as public, to cope with the complexity of risks. These arrangements should not be defined simply as inclusion per se, as they serve the purpose of framing risks (IRGC, 2017; Renn, 2008) in a way that risk-related decision-making and processes of risk assessment, risk appraisal, evaluation, management, and communication are properly done (IRGC, 2017). According to Risk Governance, actors are expected to engage rationally, working collectively to resolve problems. In the social sciences, rational action is closely tied to methodological individualism, which asserts that social phenomena are best explained by analysing how they emerge from individual actions, guided by the intentional states and motivations of those actors (Elster, 1989).

This expectation also applies to actors dealing with risk, according to Security Studies, although the emphasis is stronger on state actors, which include national governments and their agencies. However, while risk management and governance focus primarily on addressing risks through structured and objective frameworks, Security Studies extensively analyse power dynamics and balances, which are almost absent in traditional Risk Governance approaches. Security Studies theorists emphasise the unequal distribution of power and its influence on decision-making and policy implementation.

In addition, actors in Security Studies frame risks as socially constructed categories shaped by discourses, institutional practices, and the exercise of power, all influencing the understanding of risk. These actors operate within institutional assemblages and structures, shaping governmental strategies that embed risk into decision-making processes. They play a pivotal role in defining action plans to enhance governance and the resilience of referent objects—whether individuals, communities, or infrastructures—against potential threats. Moreover, these actors hold positions of power, which grant them the authority to legitimise precautionary measures and policies, particularly in response to extraordinary events. Their capacity to define what constitutes a risk and how it should be managed has significant implications for management and governance, often reinforcing power imbalances and prioritising specific agendas. In this way, risk management justifies pre-emptive actions and expands governance measures.

2.4.3 *Risk Practices in the Two Perspectives*

Risk Governance employs a range of practices focused on understanding, assessing, and managing risk, including risk appraisal, vulnerability analysis, risk assessment, risk evaluation, and risk communication (IRGC, 2017). These tools are designed to identify risk factors, mitigate potential harms, and calculate the probability of risks occurring, all in support of the overarching goal of risk governance: to manage potential risks effectively. These risk practices are often routinised and institutionalised within structures and policy processes, ensuring consistency and reliability in risk governance. Within the IRGC Framework, decision-making and related practices are typically guided by the precautionary principle, which prioritises proactive measures to prevent harm in the face of uncertainty (IRGC, 2017). This principle underscores the commitment to minimising risks before they materialise, emphasising safety and preparedness.

The increasing use of risk language in Security Studies has had a significant impact on how scholars debate security practices. Several of these practices are typical risk practices, aligned with those of the Risk Governance discipline: risk management, the precautionary principle, contingency planning, and pre-emption are a few examples. As Friis and Reichborn-Kjennerud (2016) highlight, these practices have contributed to the routinisation of security, where security measures have increasingly become risk-based practices in fields that go beyond military threats and encompass political, economic, environmental, and societal risks. These have expanded the field of research in Security Studies to include human and societal security, environmental security, and cybersecurity, drawing on constructivist and critical approaches that view security as socially constructed. As global challenges become more complex and interconnected, the distinction between security threats and risks continues to blur, necessitating more adaptive and comprehensive approaches to security governance.

The shift away from a purely realist ontology is evident in how Risk Governance practices align with normative political theory, particularly in the tradition of Habermas. Normative politics concerns the principles, values, and ideals that should guide political behaviour, institutions, and governance. Core principles such as democratic norms, the rule of law, accountability, and participatory governance serve as benchmarks for ethical political practices and communication. Security, politics, and practice are intrinsically linked, shaping the protection of national, corporate, and organisational assets. Security politics encompasses strategic decisions, policies, and laws that regulate national and international security, including cybersecurity frameworks, military defence strategies, and geopolitical conflicts. This framing often justifies heightened surveillance, stricter laws, and emergency policies.

When Risk Governance principles become instruments of government action, they also serve to legitimise securitisation. This dual role of Risk Governance highlights its paradoxical nature: on the one hand, facilitating deliberative procedures and promoting democratic participation through civic engagement, and on the other, legitimising precautionary principles, regulatory measures, and restrictions.

Ethical political leadership, transparency, and constitutionalism are essential for ensuring just governance. However, challenges such as political realism, cultural differences, authoritarianism, and economic inequality often obstruct the realisation of the Habermasian vision of Risk Governance. In such cases, Security Studies provide a more pragmatic perspective. Despite these challenges, normative politics remain a vital framework for advocating justice, ethical Risk Governance, and effective communication in both domestic and global contexts.

2.5 Conclusion

In today's international security landscape, risks are pervasive, ranging from climate change and terrorism to the proliferation of cyberattacks. If it is true that the contemporary world is becoming confused, polarised, and increasingly complex, interaction and interfaces between disciplines may help to address this challenge, especially since security and risk are nowadays informed by uncertainty and ambiguity. Security Studies and Risk Governance, though distinct, are increasingly interconnected as contemporary threats and risks evolve and become more complex and intertwined. The three interfaces we have underlined can contribute to showing where the two disciplines interconnect, although Security Studies seem to be influenced more strongly by the discipline of Risk Governance than vice versa.

Scholars from Security Studies have benefited from the introduction of the concept of risk, widened their field of study, and learned to understand

and consider the interconnections between phenomena like the meaning and implications of risk for security. Integrating risk in security presents challenges, including balancing preventive measures with civil liberties and addressing the limitations of transparency in security contexts. However, the incorporation of Risk Governance principles—whether through technocratic assessments or participatory and deliberative processes—can make security strategies more adaptive, inclusive, and effective in mitigating complex global risks.

Traditional Security Studies, rooted in state-centric approaches, have historically focused on immediate threats such as war and terrorism. Security Studies often adopt risk concepts to describe and interpret threats, particularly in terms of discourse, power, and social construction. However, they typically lack tools for operationalising or acting on risk, especially in terms of structured frameworks for decision-making. Their focus tends to be on the politics of risk—how risks are framed, who frames them, and to what end—rather than on offering practical guidance for managing uncertainty.

In contrast, Risk Governance addresses systemic uncertainties through participatory decision-making, transparency, and adaptive strategies. It emphasises stakeholder engagement, balancing expert knowledge with public discourse to enhance societal resilience. Risk Governance is also much more oriented towards acting on risk. It focuses on tools, procedures, and participatory frameworks to handle uncertainty, often in highly institutionalised settings. Further, it is more critical towards normative implications, for instance, who gets included in decision-making, how knowledge is validated, and what values underlie decisions. Risk scholars are concerned not just with how risk is analysed, but also with how those analyses are translated into governance practices and what consequences they have for legitimacy and effectiveness.

Risk Governance emphasises the inclusion of multiple stakeholders in the decision-making process to integrate diverse perspectives, fostering communication across disciplines, social groups, and institutions to develop global and complex risk management strategies. The goal is to identify and address controversies among these viewpoints, explore options for risk-reducing measures and preparedness principles, and determine whether risks should be mitigated. However, challenges remain in addressing power dynamics and asymmetric information. Disagreements among experts require reflexive discussions to align theories and methods with affected parties and foster trust between powerholders and the public or experts. Yet, they also risk creating power imbalances and conflicts of interest.

While Risk Governance focuses on managing complex risks and preventing power struggles, Security Studies critically examines power dynamics and public–expert relationships that can hinder security. In the interface concerning risk management and policymaking, intersecting Security Studies with Risk Governance approaches to risk management and policymaking allows Security Studies to offer critical insights into how risks are not only managed but also constructed, governed, and leveraged as instruments of power.

Risk Governance continues to define, conceptualise, and address risks both theoretically and practically, forming the foundation for political measures and strategies to reduce vulnerabilities. Risk Governance has benefited from elaborations of the risk concept from Risk Science, with its substantial contributions within the field of risk analysis, Risk Governance, and politics of risk. Although Security Studies have not been engaged in the processes behind risk analysis, risk evaluation, risk assessment, and risk management as much as Risk Governance, we argue that this knowledge has greatly benefited the advances in Security Studies to understand risk.

The interface in risk understanding shows, however, that there is a need to deepen the two fields' understanding of uncertainty. To address this issue, scholars must develop clearer frameworks for grappling with uncertainty, particularly in high-stakes areas such as climate change adaptation. Governance models must strike a balance between technical expertise and democratic legitimacy, avoiding top-down decisions disguised as neutral risk management. While the integration of risk frameworks could improve societal resilience, this potential remains underexplored and demands greater attention in both research and practice. Applying participatory principles from Risk Governance in the realm of security could strengthen both the effectiveness and legitimacy of policy responses. Ultimately, ongoing reflexive dialogue among scholars and practitioners is essential to align risk conceptualisations, expose blind spots, and critically engage with the power dynamics that shape how risks are defined, governed, and communicated.

References

Aradau, C., Lobo-Guerrero, L., & Van Munster, R. (2008). Security, technologies of risk, and the political: Guest editors' introduction. *Security Dialogue, 39*(2–3), 147–154.

Aradau, C., & Van Munster, R. (2007). Governing terrorism through risk: Taking precautions, (un)knowing the future. *European Journal of International Relations, 13*(1), 89–115.

Aradau, C., & Van Munster, R. (2008). Insuring terrorism, assuring subjects, ensuring normality: The politics of risk after 9/11. *Alternatives, 33*(2), 191–210.

Aven, T. (2010). On how to define, understand and describe risk. *Reliability Engineering and System Safety, 95*, 623–631.

Aven, T. (2020). *The science of risk analysis: Foundation and practice.* Routledge.

Aven, T., & Krohn, B. S. (2014). A new perspective on how to understand, assess and manage risk and the unforeseen. *Reliability Engineering and System Safety, 121*, 1–10.

Aven, T., & Thekdi, S. (2022). *Risk science: An introduction.* Routledge.

Beck, U. (1992). *Risk society: Towards a new modernity.* Sage.

Beck, U. (1999). *World risk society.* Polity Press.

Beck, U., & Wehling, P. (2012). The politics of non-knowing: An emerging area of social and political conflict in reflexive modernity. In P. Baert & F. Domínguez Rubio (Eds.), *The politics of knowledge* (pp. 33–57). Routledge.

Bengtsson, L., Borg, S., & Rhinard, M. (2018). European security and early warning systems: From risks to threats in the European Union's health security sector. *European Security, 27*(1), 20–40.

Bigo, D. (2002). Security and immigration: Towards a critique of the governmentality of unease. *Alternatives, 27*(1), 63–92.

Bigo, D., & Tsoukala, A. (Eds.). (2008). *Terror, insecurity and liberty: Illiberal practices of liberal regimes after 9/11.* Routledge.

Bonholm, A., & Corvellec, H. (2011). A relational theory of risk. *Journal of Risk Research, 14*(1–2), 175–190.

Buzan, B., & Hansen, L. (2009). *The evolution of international security studies.* Cambridge University Press.

Corry, O. (2012). Securitisation and 'riskification': Second-order security and the politics of climate change. *Millennium: Journal of International Studies, 40*(2), 235–258. https://doi.org/10.1177/0305829811419444

Dean, M. (1999). *Governmentality: Power and rule in modern society.* Sage Publications.

Elster, J. (1989). Nuts and Bolts for the Social Sciences. Cambridge University Press.

Foucault M. (1980). The confession of the flesh. In C. Gordon (Ed.), *Power/knowledge selected interviews and other writings 1972–1977* (pp. 194–228). Longman.

Foucault, M. (1997). What is enlightenment? In S. Lotringer (Ed.), *The politics of truth* (pp. 101–134). Semiotext(e).

Friis, K., & Reichborn-Kjennerud, E. (2016). From cyber threats to cyber risks. In K. Friis & J. Ringsmose (Eds.), *Conflict in cyberspace: Theoretical, strategic and legal perspectives* (pp. 27–44). Routledge.

Gad, U. P., & Petersen, K. L. (2011). Concepts of politics in securitization studies. *Security Dialogue, 42*(4–5), 315–328. https://doi.org/10.1177/0967010611418716

Habermas, J. (2018). *Philosophical introductions. Five approaches to communicative reason.* Polity Press.

Huysmans, J. (2002). Defining social constructivism in Security Studies: The normative dilemma of writing security. *Alternatives, 27,* 41–62.

Huysmans, J. (2011). What's in an act? On security speech acts and little security nothings. *Security Dialogue, 42*(4–5), 371–383.

IRGC International Risk Governance Council. (2017). *Introduction to the IRGC risk governance framework, revised version.* EPFL International Risk Governance Centre.

Katzenstein, P. J., & Seybert, L. A. (2018). Uncertainty, risk, power and the limits of international relations theory. In P. J. Katzenstein & L. A. Seybert (Eds.), *Protean power: Exploring the uncertain and unexpected in world politics* (pp. 27–56). Cambridge University Press.

Kessler, O. (2010). Risk. In J. P. Burgess (Ed.), *The Routledge handbook of new Security Studies* (pp. 17–26). Routledge.

Kirk, J. (2020). From threat to risk? Exceptionalism and logics of health security. *International Studies Quarterly, 64,* 266–276. https://doi.org/10.1093/isq/sqaa021

Lupton, D. (2023). *Risk.* Routledge.

McSweeney, B. (1999). *Security, identity and interests: A sociology of international relations.* Cambridge University Press.

Michaels, J. H. (2024). Deterrence studies: A field still in progress. *Journal of Strategic Studies, 47*(6–7), 1058–1079. https://doi.org/10.1080/01402390.2024.2417388

Petersen, K. L. (2008). Terrorism: When risk meets security. *Alternatives 33*(2), 173–190.

Petersen, K. L. (2011). Risk analysis – A field within Security Studies? *European Journal of International Relations, 18*(4), 693–717.

Petersen, K. L. (2016). Risk and security. In M. Dunn Cavelty & T. Balzacq (Eds.), *Routledge handbook on Security Studies* (2nd ed., pp. 117–125). Routledge.

Rasmussen, M. V. (2006). *The risk society at war: Terror, technology and strategy in the twenty-first century.* Cambridge University Press.

Rathbun, B. C. (2007). Uncertain about uncertainty: Understanding the multiple meanings of a crucial concept in international relations theory. *International Studies Quarterly, 51*, 533–557.

Renn, O. (2008). *Risk Governance: Coping with uncertainty in a complex world*. Routledge.

Rosa, E. A. (1998). Metatheoretical foundations for post-normal risk. *Journal of Risk Research, 1*(1), 15–44. https://doi.org/10.1080/136698798377303

Salter, M. B. (2008). Securitization and desecuritization: A dramaturgical analysis of the Canadian Transport Security Authority. *Journal of International Relations and Development, 11*(4), 321–349.

Tierney, K. J. (2014). *The Social Roots of Risk: Producing disasters, promoting resilience*. Stanford Business Books.

van Asselt, M. B. A., & Renn, O. (2011). Risk Governance. *Journal of Risk Research, 14*(4), 431–449.

van Munster, R. (2005). *Logics of security: The Copenhagen school, risk management*. Political Science Publications, 10. Faculty of Social Sciences, University of Southern Denmark.

Wæver, O. (2011). Politics, security, theory. *Security Dialogue, 42*(4–5), 465–480.

Williams, M. J. (2008). (In)Security studies, reflexive modernization and the risk society. *Cooperation and Conflict, 43(1)*, 57–79.

CHAPTER 3

Systemic Risk Governance for Disaster Risk Management and Climate Change Adaptation

Pia-Johanna Schweizer, Benjamin Hofbauer, and Paul Einhäupl

Abstract Systemic risks, marked by cascading, interconnected effects across ecological, social, and economic domains, pose unprecedented challenges for climate change adaptation and disaster risk management. Climate change acts as a risk multiplier, intensifying the complexity, uncertainty, and transboundary nature of these risks. This chapter explores how systemic risk governance must evolve to confront these challenges,

Pia-Johanna Schweizer and Benjamin Hofbauer acknowledge funding from the "DIsaster Resilience for Extreme ClimaTe Events providing interoperable Data, models, communication and governance" (DIRECTED) project, an Innovation Action under the Civil Security for Society, Disaster-Resilient Societies programme of Horizon Europe (2022–2026). Grant #101073978.

P.-J. Schweizer (✉) • B. Hofbauer • P. Einhäupl
RIFS Research Institute for Sustainability at GFZ Helmholtz Centre for Geosciences, Potsdam, Germany
e-mail: pia-johanna.schweizer@rifs-potsdam.de;
benjamin.hofbauer@rifs-potsdam.de; paul.einhaeupl@rifs-potsdam.de

C. Morsut (ed.), *Adapting to Climate Change*,
https://doi.org/10.1007/978-3-032-07136-1_3

emphasising the need for integrated, anticipatory, and ethically grounded approaches. Drawing on systems thinking, systemic risks are conceptualised as emergent phenomena driven by feedback loops, interdependencies, and tipping points. It is argued that governance should be grounded in reflection, iteration, and deliberation to ensure evidence-based risk analysis, fair decision-making processes, and equitable outcomes. Ethical considerations are central, as risk governance decisions are value-laden and context-dependent. The Horizon Europe project DIRECTED serves as an exemplar, demonstrating how innovations can enhance resilience, bridge local and systemic perspectives, and support continuous learning in risk governance.

Keywords Climate change adaptation • Disaster risk management • Ethics • Risk governance • Systemic risks • Stakeholder engagement • Systems thinking

3.1 Introduction

Systemic risk, characterised by cascading impacts that spread within and across systems and sectors, presents profound challenges in the context of climate change adaptation. These impacts are transmitted through the movements of people, goods, capital, and information across regions, countries, and continents (Lawrence et al., 2020; Renn et al., 2022). When compounded by underlying vulnerabilities, such as socio-economic inequalities, degraded ecosystems, and fragile infrastructure, these cascading effects can lead to system collapse, with potentially existential consequences over short- and long-term horizons (Centeno et al., 2015; Helbing, 2013; Lawrence et al., 2024).

Climate change acts as a risk multiplier, exacerbating both the frequency and intensity of extreme weather events and stressing critical interdependencies across ecological, economic, technical, and social systems (IPCC, 2023). For example, extreme weather events not only impact food production but also disrupt supply chains, financial markets, and health systems, illustrating the deeply interconnected nature of modern risk landscapes (Carter et al., 2021). Therefore, understanding the root causes and transmission mechanisms of systemic risks, whether biophysical or societal, is imperative for developing adaptation strategies. A systemic risk lens demands that adaptation efforts move beyond isolated interventions towards more integrated and anticipatory approaches

(Boyd & Juhola, 2015). Building resilience thus requires identifying effective leverage points within systems, fostering adaptive capacities across scales, and embedding flexibility into governance mechanisms (Folke et al., 2016; Hynes et al., 2020). This includes enhancing early warning systems, investing in resilient infrastructure, promoting social equity, and encouraging cross-sectoral collaboration. Risk governance frameworks must evolve to accommodate the inherent uncertainty, non-linearity, and transboundary nature of systemic risks (Renn et al., 2022; Schweizer, 2021; Schweizer & Juhola, 2024). Moreover, political and societal responses play a crucial role in either attenuating or amplifying systemic risks (Schweizer et al., 2022). The key drivers of systemic risks spring from the interdependencies and relationships among various actors and elements in a given system, and how the failure or inadequate functioning of one part of the system impacts the entire system. Maladaptive responses, such as protectionist trade measures following climate-induced crop failures, can further entrench vulnerabilities and propagate risks globally (Keohane, 2010; Keohane & Victor, 2016). Therefore, fostering inclusive, transparent, and reflexive governance structures is essential to navigating the complex interactions between climate change adaptation and systemic risk management.

Integrating systemic risk thinking into climate change adaptation strategies is not merely a conceptual refinement, but also a practical necessity. By addressing the interdependencies and cascading effects that characterise contemporary risk landscapes, societies can enhance resilience, safeguard critical systems, and better prepare for an uncertain climatic future.

The chapter proceeds with Sect. 3.2, giving a general overview of systemic risk governance. In so doing, it first explores the relationship between governance and risk, outlining how risk governance has evolved towards including processes of deliberation and participation. The section then links the discussion surrounding risk governance to systems thinking, underscoring how systems thinking is an insightful conceptual lens for the exploration of systemic risks and their governance. In addition, ethical implications of systemic risk governance are highlighted. Sect. 3.3 gives an overview of the Horizon Europe project DIRECTED, wherein the principles and concepts of systemic risk governance laid out in the previous section have been applied to support disaster risk management and climate change adaptation strategies. The conclusion highlights some of the limitations that come with systemic risk governance approaches and points out possible ways forward.

3.2 Governance for Systemic Risks

Several challenges for the governance of systemic risks have been identified in the literature. Systemic risks (1) are transboundary or cross-sectoral in the scope of their consequences leading to multiple ripple effects; (2) are highly interconnected and intertwined, leading to complex causal structures, high uncertainty, and major interpretative ambiguities; (3) are non-linear in their cause–effect relationships that come with tipping points; (4) are stochastic in their effect structure, leading to increased uncertainty that is difficult or impossible to characterise by statistical confidence intervals; and (5) tend to have a lag in policymaking which is at least partially due to social processes of risk perception (Renn et al., 2022; Schweizer, 2021; Schweizer & Renn, 2019; Schweizer et al., 2022; Sillmann et al., 2022). Due to the complexity, uncertainty, and ambiguity that characterise systemic risks, an evidence-based approach is essential for guiding effective decision-making including collaborative governance strategies. Such approaches must be guided by ethical considerations, exploring diverse normative frameworks. From these interlinked implications, i.e. procedural, scientific, and normative, arise a set of practical requirements for governing systemic risks.

3.2.1 *Risk Governance*

The catastrophic potential of systemic risks demands urgent action. Yet, complexity, uncertainty, and ambiguity challenge both science and politics, as Chap. 2 pointed out. These challenges raise pressing questions, such as what the goals of governance are, which course of action is appropriate, effective, and efficient, who sets the course and what is their mandate, and what the roles of science, civil society, the economy, etc. are. Governance engages with such questions. Aiming to offer answers by rethinking the concept of governance, this section explores how governance theory and practice have evolved to meet the demands of systemic risk contexts. In this sense, governance reflects the shift in how authority, influence, and coordination are understood. These shifts are 'conceptualized in three different directions: upward (to the regional, transnational, intergovernmental, and global), downward (to the local, regional, and the metropolitan), and horizontally (to private and civil spheres of authority)' (Levi-Faur, 2012, p. 7). Thus, governance marks a change in the meaning of government, introducing new processes of governing, altered conditions of ordered rule, and different methods by which society is managed

(Rhodes, 2012). Governance also reflects ideological and cultural shifts, particularly towards individualism and the market as the dominant mechanism for resource allocation (Pierre, 2000). Importantly, as Levi-Faur emphasises, governance is not a unified theory. It is not a single field of study, nor does it provide a comprehensive causal framework for understanding politics, economics, and society (Levi-Faur, 2012). Nonetheless, four general themes are associated with governance: it may be seen as a structure, a process, a mechanism, or a strategy. As Levi-Faur explains: 'As a structure, governance signifies the architecture of formal and informal institutions; as the process it signifies the dynamics and steering functions involved in lengthy never-ending processes of policymaking; as a mechanism it signifies institutional procedures of decision-making, of compliance and of control (or instruments); finally, as a strategy it signifies the actors' efforts to govern and manipulate the design of institutions and mechanisms in order to shape choice and preferences' (Levi-Faur, 2012, p. 8).

This conceptual flexibility allows governance to speak to diverse contexts, particularly in relation to systemic risk and climate risk. Critical reflections of risk discourses have highlighted the importance of including a broader range of societal actors in governance (Fisher, 2012). In this context, risk governance refers to participatory, deliberative processes involving stakeholders and the public (see Chap. 2). These processes become vital sources of democratic legitimacy for risk-related decisions, drawing on extended peer, stakeholder, and public communities (Klinke & Renn, 2012, 2021). Risk governance, therefore, goes beyond simply linking risk analysis, i.e. the systematic process of understanding risk, with risk communication, i.e. the exchange of risk-related information among regulators, stakeholders, media, and the public. Risk governance includes the totality of actors, rules, conventions, processes, and mechanisms concerned with how relevant risk information is collected, analysed and communicated, and how management decisions are taken (IRGC, 2005, 2018).

Stakeholder and public engagement in risk governance has long been advocated, supported by three primary arguments: (1) substantive, (2) instrumental, and (3) normative (Fiorino, 1990; Stirling, 2006).

1. The substantive argument suggests that including a diversity of perspectives enhances the quality of information and decisions. Stakeholders and the public contribute crucial insights from both scientific and non-scientific knowledge systems (Fischhoff, 1995).

2. The instrumental argument holds that participation can improve the implementation and acceptance of decisions (Beierle, 1999; Slovic, 1993). In this view, governance becomes more effective.
3. The normative argument sees participation as a means to address conflict, build dialogue in polarised contexts, promote fairness, give a voice to the marginalised (Innes & Booher, 2004), and empower citizens (Arnstein, 1969). It can foster social cohesion and trust (National Research Council, 2008).

As a result, stakeholder engagement and public participation are standard features of many risk governance efforts (Webler & Tuler, 2021). Risk governance has become an 'inclusive and participatory activity that integrates various stakeholder perspectives, engages in the co-generation of practical knowledge, and resolves contingencies by developing discrete scenarios that translate different concerns and positions in negotiable and communicable narratives' (Klinke & Renn, 2021, p. 3).

This development has led to the concept of inclusive risk governance (Renn & Klinke, 2012; Renn & Schweizer, 2009). Inclusive risk governance integrates extended peer communities, stakeholders, and the public into the decision-making process. It also emphasises the distribution of responsibility among these actors. This approach supports the deliberative and participatory turn in risk governance, where responsibilities are shared and differentiated among those with relevant authority and those directly affected. Participation and deliberation are essential components of this approach.

Unlike traditional models, which rely on decisions made primarily by government agencies or private entities, inclusive risk governance draws its legitimacy and effectiveness from three key sources: (1) the inclusion of diverse types of knowledge, (2) the active involvement of networks and communities, and (3) public deliberation based on open and inclusive discussions about the risk issues (Klinke & Renn, 2021). To address the interconnected and evolving nature of systemic risks, risk governance must thus be supported by analytical approaches capable of capturing complexity, uncertainty, and ambiguity, as well as the integration of stakeholders. Systems thinking provides such a foundation by enabling the structured analysis of interdependencies, feedback loops, and cascading effects.

3.2.2 Systems Thinking

Systems thinking provides a structured approach for analysing interdependent, dynamic systems and has become essential for understanding and governing systemic risks (Schweizer, 2021; Schweizer & Juhola, 2024). In the context of systemic risks, systems thinking should be understood as a conceptual lens for exploring relations between interconnected factors from multiple perspectives, rather than as a rigid set of tools and methods (Williams & Hummelbrunner, 2010). Because of its applicability and relevance across practical and scientific domains, systems thinking is inherently inter- and transdisciplinary. The conceptual roots of systems thinking lie in mid-twentieth-century systems theory. Researchers from different disciplinary angles contributed to a more holistic understanding of systems as interdependent, self-organising structures (Mele et al., 2010). As a part of this development, Forrester (1961) developed system dynamics to analyse feedback-driven processes in industrial systems. Sterman (2000) advanced system dynamics for policy design, clarifying how decisions interact with system structures over time. Within system dynamics, causal loop diagrams emerged as qualitative tools to visualise feedback mechanisms and foster shared understanding among stakeholders (Sterman, 2000). Since they make interdependencies visible, causal loop diagrams facilitate the identification of key variables, leverage points, and potential cascading effects. Systems thinking also informs concepts such as resilience and adaptation. Holling (1973) introduced the concept of resilience in ecological systems, defining it as the capacity to absorb disturbances while maintaining core functions and structures. In this context, adaptation contributes to resilience: adaptive measures enhance a system's ability to reorganise under stress, reinforcing its persistence (Folke et al., 2010; Fraccascia et al., 2018). Resilience has since become central to systemic risk analysis, highlighting the importance of coping mechanisms in dynamic, uncertain conditions (Renn et al., 2011).

Systems thinking is essential for the assessment and governance of systemic risks since it provides the conceptual and methodological frame for engaging with complexity. Systemic risks are characterised by non-linear propagation, interdependencies, and cross-sectoral feedback, all of which undermine the predictive capacity of linear models (Renn et al., 2022). Systems thinking enables a structured analysis of these features by mapping feedback mechanisms, identifying critical linkages, and informing governance strategies accordingly (Sterman, 2000). Moreover, identifying functional roles within a system, their relations and dynamics, needs an integrated approach which helps reveal potential tipping points or vulnerabilities (Otto et al., 2020; Renn et al., 2022). Clarifying these roles is essential for enabling governance to utilise adaptive capacities. By delineating system boundaries and subsystem interactions, systems thinking improves the ability to assess potential impacts of interventions and decisions. Its integrative approach fosters cross-sectoral and cross-scale analysis and coordination, particularly in fields such as disaster risk management and climate change adaptation (Centeno et al., 2015).

Nevertheless, the application of systems thinking to systemic risk analysis is not without limitations, two of which should be explicitly mentioned. First, setting system boundaries, especially in large-scale, interconnected societal systems, can result in marginalisation of cultural, regional, or normative perspectives (Williams & Hummelbrunner, 2010). This raises ethical concerns around who defines the system, and whose perspectives are prioritised. Second, systems thinking often relies on data-informed models, which can inadvertently reproduce existing data biases and overlook marginalised knowledge systems (Carvalho et al., 2025). Furthermore, systems thinking does not inherently address questions of accountability. Accountability, as a value-laden concept, must be defined through legal and procedural frameworks rather than derived from systemic logic alone (Williams & Hummelbrunner, 2010).

To mitigate these limitations, reflexivity should be embedded in systemic risk assessment and governance (Schweizer & Juhola, 2024). Through analytical iteration, systems thinking offers a useful foundation for integrating reflection into modelling processes, encouraging pluralistic perspectives and critical awareness of normative assumptions. In sum, systems thinking is not value-neutral. Rather, it depends on the perspectives, boundaries, and priorities defined by those who apply it. Therefore, ethical considerations must be systematically integrated into the assessment and governance of systemic risks.

3.2.3 *Ethics and Systemic Risk Governance*

Crucial factors for the assessment and evaluation of systemic risk governance measures are the ethical implications that such measure sentail. Especially when it comes to the systemic adaptation to climate change and climate risks, questions of justice and equity abound (Byskov et al., 2021; Heyward, 2017). Both the nature of systemic risks and the process of governing systemic risks lead to normative questions that require deliberation and engagement. Risk itself is by definition a value-laden concept (Hansson, 2013, see also Chap. 2), describing the potential consequence of an action or event for something that people value. Systemic risks further introduce important challenges regarding justice and equity considerations throughout the governance process. In particular, a variety of justice issues arise in the context of governing systemic risks. Following the common distinction between procedural and distributive justice in political philosophy (Rawls, 1999),[1] governing systemic risks needs to account for a fair procedure throughout the decision-making process, as well as an equitable distribution of benefits and burdens in its outcome (Taebi, 2017). Ensuring equitable distribution entails that decision-makers consider how the imposition of risks should be evaluated (Hayenhjelm & Wolff, 2012). From the perspective of systemic risks as continuous, dynamic processes, such an evaluation is complex and requires iterative deliberation (Hofbauer, 2023).

Apart from the governance outcome of systemic risks accounting for justice, the decision-making process itself is also of critical ethical relevance. In line with philosophy and ethics scholarship, procedural justice entails meaningful and equitable participation (Habermas, 2004), and those outcomes are based on fair procedures (Nozick, 1974). Importantly, some strands within the non-ideal tradition of justice thinking, that underscores the importance of accounting for existing injustices in any theoretical undertaking (Valentini, 2012), highlight the need for recognitional approaches and a systemic understanding of societal relationships (Fraser & Honneth, 2003; Young, 2011; Whyte, 2011). These approaches establish the ethical basis for meaningful participation and recognition, stipulating the necessity to account for the historical and systemic discrimination faced by many non-white, Indigenous, low-income, elderly, and other marginalised communities. Such thinking provides insights for the distributional and procedural aspects of systemic risks, especially when it comes to inclusive and participatory governance frameworks (Renn & Schweizer, 2020). Ultimately, what kind of function or purpose the system in question serves, as well as for who it serves that function or purpose for,

[1] There are other ways to define and categorise various justice conceptions (Miller, 2025). For the purpose of this brief introduction, however, we believe the procedural/distributional distinction to suffice.

and why a given risk matters to them, sets the empirical basis for a variety of normative deliberations that require meaningful public participation.

3.3 Systemic Risk Governance, Disaster Risk Management, and Climate Change Adaptation: Lessons from the DIRECTED Project

While systems thinking provides the conceptual tools to analyse complexity, and ethical reflection addresses the normative implications of systemic risks, these insights must be translated into practical governance approaches. Effective governance of systemic risks requires the integration of systems thinking and ethical reflection into practical, inclusive strategies. Systemic risks, associated with complexity, uncertainty, and cascading effects, often resemble *black swan* events that are difficult to anticipate or fully understand (Taleb, 2010). Addressing these risks demands ongoing reflection, adaptability, and resilience, as well as a governance approach that evolves with new evidence and shifting priorities. Systems thinking provides tools to analyse interconnections and feedback loops within dynamic systems, helping identify leverage points for intervention. However, it must be applied reflectively, as it can reinforce biases through too narrow system boundaries. Ethical considerations in governance emphasise distributive and procedural justice, inclusivity, and recognition of historically disadvantaged groups. Furthermore, systemic risk governance calls for multi-level, participatory, and deliberative processes. Public engagement and stakeholder participation are essential for building legitimacy, ensuring fairness, and supporting effective decision-making. Systemic risks increasingly shape the global risk landscape, and climate-induced disasters have become emblematic of the urgent need for integrated and adaptive governance approaches (Sillmann et al., 2022; World Economic Forum, 2024). With extreme weather events on the rise, disaster risk management as well as climate change adaptation strategies become a focal point for the investigation and governance of systemic risks.

Climate-induced disasters, whether sudden-onset events like hurricanes and floods, or slow-onset phenomena like drought and sea-level rise, are increasingly interconnected through complex feedbacks across social, environmental, and technological systems (IPCC, 2023; Lawrence et al., 2024). Disasters are no longer isolated events but are capable of triggering cascading failures across critical infrastructures, economies, and governance systems (Gill & Malamud, 2016; Groundstroem & Juhola, 2021;

Helbing, 2013; Lawrence et al., 2020). The Fukushima Daiichi nuclear disaster (2011), triggered by an earthquake and tsunami, exemplifies how a single geophysical event can evolve into a multi-sector systemic crisis (Aven & Renn, 2020). Similarly, climate-amplified wildfires not only destroy ecosystems but also degrade air quality, disrupt energy supplies, and cause displacement (Ducros et al., 2024; Lucas, 2022).

3.3.1 The DIRECTED Project: A Brief Overview

Building on the insight that systemic risk governance requires broad and meaningful participation, the Risk-Tandem Framework (Parviainen et al., 2025) outlines a transferable and scalable approach towards disaster risk management as well as climate change adaptation. The approach was developed in the context of the Horizon Europe project DIRECTED, funded by the European Commission. DIRECTED aims to reduce vulnerability to extreme weather events and foster disaster-resilient societies by promoting interoperability between disaster risk management and climate change adaptation. At its core, DIRECTED aims to assess, improve, and, where possible, integrate various disaster risk management and climate change adaptation processes throughout Europe. The DIRECTED project deploys a Real-World Laboratory approach for facilitating co-production and applying its key innovations, the Risk-Tandem Framework and the Data Fabric. These innovations are put into practice in four European regions, namely, the Emilia Romagna region in Italy, the Capital Region of Denmark, the Rhine-Erft region in Germany, and the Danube region, which covers multiple countries, e.g., Austria and Hungary (Schröter et al., 2024). The DIRECTED Real-World Laboratories are composed of local stakeholders, governance and administrative practitioners, scientists, and Real-World Laboratory hosts, i.e. project partners who serve as intermediaries between the DIRECTED consortium and the local communities. This setup allows for continuous engagement and learning, both for consortium members and for hosts and stakeholders (Cumiskey et al., 2025). The project uses a co creative methodology, wherein the research questions as well as the methods are co-developed alongside the affected stakeholders and practitioners (Bharwani et al., 2024). This ensures that the outcomes of the project are solution-oriented and tailored to address the real-world problems of stakeholders.

3.3.2 Merging Systemic Risk Governance, Disaster Risk Management, and Climate Change Adaptation Through the DIRECTED Risk-Tandem Framework

Conventional disaster risk management often relies on historical data and risk maps based on past disaster events. However, systemic risks necessitate anticipatory reflection on emerging hazards, novel threat combinations, and new vulnerabilities increased by climate change impacts, socio-technical transformations, and financial mechanisms (UNDRR, 2019, 2023, 2025). Scenario planning, foresight exercises, and stress testing of critical systems have increasingly become standard practices to explore complex, low-probability, high-impact risks (Abdelhakim et al., 2024; Bourgeois et al., 2017; Döll & Romero-Lankao, 2017). With an ever-changing risk landscape, it is crucial to ensure a continuous learning process that can be adapted to changing circumstances. Accounting for this dynamism, the disaster risk management and climate change adaptation strategies that are explored and sought to be improved in the DIRECTED project via the Risk-Tandem Framework are built around reflection, iteration, and deliberation (Parviainen et al., 2025).

Reflection is crucial due to the unpredictable nature of systemic risks, which often involve tipping points and cascading effects that are difficult to anticipate. This implies that the governance process must be designed and implemented in a way that explicitly acknowledges and critically assesses the conceptual and methodological tools on which it relies, as well as the inherent uncertainties associated with extreme weather events. For example, the Risk-Tandem Framework draws on a number of existing approaches, combining societal vulnerability with risk finance tools, as well as co-creation and modelling approaches. Such a variety of tools results in a substantially rich picture of potential systemic risks, supporting more effective disaster risk management and climate change adaptation. At the same time, the diverse concepts underlying this framework need to be brought together through a shared conceptual language. For example, insights from a social vulnerability analysis may conflict with recommendations from a risk financing perspective.

With the reflective dimension in mind, governing systemic risks in the disaster risk management and climate change adaptation context also requires iteration in order to allow for the continuous restructuring of the management strategies. Iteration is crucial, since it makes room for the fine-tuning of a given disaster risk management and climate change adaptation strategy. The needs of stakeholders and affected people vary across regions, and the local context is paramount for the efficient and sustainable handling of systemic risks. Accordingly, the Risk-Tandem Framework is applied iteratively, explicitly allowing for a consistent monitoring, evaluation, and learning process (Parviainen et al., 2025).

Iteration offers a segue into deliberation. Deliberative, inclusive governance is essential for systemic risk management, ensuring that diverse perspectives, local knowledge, and vulnerable voices inform disaster risk management strategies (Klinke & Renn, 2021; Nalau et al., 2021). Participation enhances legitimacy, equity, and the substantive quality of decisions (Fiorino, 1990; Arnstein, 1969). In the context of systemic risk governance, inclusion is essential for both epistemic and ethical reasons. Epistemically, involving a broad range of stakeholders, e.g. through participatory governance frameworks, brings in more diverse perspectives, leading to richer and more comprehensive information. Ethically, inclusive governance is grounded in the premise that all those affected by a decision should have a say in the governance process leading towards decisions. This means ensuring meaningful participation in decision-making processes. The Risk-Tandem Framework addresses this by emphasising co-creation in both risk governance and agenda setting. It also emphasises the importance of transparent communication of uncertainties, cascading effects, and potential trade-offs. While uncertainty cannot be eliminated, it can be navigated by participation and deliberation, enhancing trust and informed decision-making (van der Sluijs et al., 2005; Renn, 2008).

Within the Risk-Tandem Framework, continuous stakeholder engagement, e.g. by through collaboration on key research questions, ensures the building and maintaining of a trusting relationship. Crucially, this collaboration is not just a unidirectional sharing of information but rather framed as a communal effort to build a strong, locally relevant research project. By default, this approach necessitates open communication between researchers and local actors to come to a shared understanding of the issue. Among stakeholders, the Risk-Tandem Framework further helps institutionalising communication platforms and shared knowledge repositories to enable interested community members to track the decision-making process regarding disaster risk management and climate change adaptation in their region.

3.3.3 *Managing Information Through the Data Fabric*

While striving for reflection, iteration, and deliberation is crucial for sustainable and effective systemic risk governance, it requires a thorough and cohesive data management strategy to facilitate data and modelling interoperability. Thus, apart from the immediate governance dimensions expressed in the Risk-Tandem Framework, the DIRECTED project also develops a framework for the interoperability of datasets and models to improve decision-making on systemic risks. The Data Fabric is a reference framework that accommodates the diversity of datasets and modelling approaches used throughout different organisations and across multiple national boundaries. It provides a data infrastructure to enable stakeholders to consolidate and connect relevant data sources, models, and information products across disaster risk management and climate change adaptation application domains and institutional operating systems and languages (Schröter et al., 2024). The Data Fabric plays a key complementary role to the governance and institutional leverage points identified by means of the Risk-Tandem Framework. It offers the modelling expertise needed to support well-informed and verifiable decisions. At the same time, the Data Fabric relies on the dynamic, solution-oriented processes of the Risk-Tandem Framework to ensure it focuses on societally relevant questions.

Combining the strategies of the Risk-Tandem Framework and the Data Fabric also accounts for the volatility of systemic risks. Systemic risks evolve dynamically, making fixed, one-off disaster risk management plans obsolete. Iterative governance emphasises continuous learning, allowing disaster policies and actions to adapt to changing knowledge, conditions, and social values (Folke et al., 2005; Kuhlmann et al., 2019). Accordingly, adaptation that seeks to build resilience in a multi-risk context of high uncertainty needs to rebuild, adjust, and learn post-event. A way of ensuring that these rebuilding efforts are sustainable in the long run is by tapping into local knowledge and building on community feedback, as well as continuously updating and integrating climate data.

3.4 Conclusion

The systemic nature of climate risks calls for governance approaches grounded in reflection, iteration, and deliberation. By integrating disaster risk management and climate change adaptation through systemic risk thinking, policymakers and practitioners can enhance societal resilience, anticipate cascading failures, and craft adaptive strategies capable of navigating the uncertainties of a rapidly changing climate. In doing so, disaster risk management and climate change adaptation become not just mechanisms for crisis response but cornerstones of proactive, sustainable, and inclusive climate change adaptation.

Through the DIRECTED project and its Risk-Tandem Framework, this chapter illustrates how reflection, iteration, and deliberation can support more adaptive and inclusive approaches to risk governance. Systems thinking provides tools for mapping interdependencies, anticipating tipping points, and identifying leverage points for intervention. Ethical reflection ensures that governance processes account for distributive and procedural justice, recognise marginalised perspectives, and navigate the value-laden nature of risk.

Nonetheless, while systemic risk governance is a crucial addition to the toolkit of managing growing risks through extreme weather events driven by climate change, it also has important caveats that require careful consideration and reflection, e.g. regarding sensitivity to contextual parameters when applied at scale. As analytical approaches are scaled up, marginalised needs and perspectives of vulnerable groups may become obscured by the increasing emphasis on generalisability at larger scales. This chapter accordingly emphasises the need for the integration of ethical reflection and normative decision-making into the process of systemic risk analysis, to avoid the reification of existing inequities.

A similar drawback can be noted concerning participation. The approaches laid out here are steered towards being normatively reflective, taking social justice issues and equity procedurally into account. However, given the reliance and immediate relationship with local needs, issues of equity and inclusion might slip into the background due to other priorities. At the same time, participation might be turned into a window dressing exercise, wherein ensuring that everyone's voice is heard is more akin to ticking a box rather than having meaningful impact. For this reason, it is necessary to set procedural guardrails, including ethical discourse as an integral piece to the application of deliberative systemic risk governance.

These critical reflections are only two examples of the issues that might arise in the context of systemic risk governance and the application of its principles. This highlights the need for more methodological work, developing means to account for the structurally owed risks that drive existing systemic risks. Importantly, risk scholars in the field need to grapple with the socio-political implications of building resilient and adaptive communities. Adaptation to climate change is not a politically neutral undertaking. With this in mind, the approach and concepts presented here should pave the way to further invigorate and inspire the conversation surrounding disaster risk management and climate change adaptation.

References

Abdelhakim, D., Stevance, A.-S., Bridgewater, P., Sullivan, L., Newlands, M., Barrow, S., Rengel-Gonçalves, A., Datta, R., Luga, W., Lazurko, A., Pintér, L., Schweizer, V., Gluckman, P., Sridhar, H., Saner, M., Hinwood, A., Jabbour, J., Gutiérrez-Espeleta, E. E., & Mangalagiu, D. (2024). *A guide to anticipation: Working paper on tools and methods of horizon scanning and foresight.* International Science Council. https://doi.org/10.24948/2024.10

Arnstein, S. R. (1969). A ladder of citizen participation. *Journal of the American Institute of Planners, 35*(4), 216–224. https://doi.org/10.1080/01944366908977225

Aven, T., & Renn, O. (2020). Some foundational issues related to risk governance and different types of risks. *Journal of Risk Research, 23*(9), 1121–1134.

Beierle, T. C. (1999). Using social goals to evaluate public participation in environmental decisions. *Review of Policy Research, 16*(3–4), 75–103. https://doi.org/10.1111/j.1541-1338.1999.tb00879.x

Bharwani, S., Gerger Swartling, Å., André, K., Santos Santos, T. F., Salamanca, A., Biskupska, N., Takama, T., Järnberg, L., & Liu, A. (2024). Co-designing in Tandem: Case study journeys to inspire and guide climate services. *Climate Services, 35*, 100503. https://doi.org/10.1016/j.cliser.2024.100503

Bourgeois, R., Penunia, E., Bisht, S., & Boruk, D. (2017). Foresight for all: Co-elaborative scenario building and empowerment. *Technological Forecasting and Social Change, 124*, 178–188. https://doi.org/10.1016/j.techfore.2017.04.018

Boyd, E., & Juhola, S. (2015). Adaptive climate change governance for urban resilience. *Urban Studies, 52*(7), 1234–1264. https://doi.org/10.1177/0042098014527483

Byskov, M. F., Hyams, K., Satyal, P., Anguelovski, I., Benjamin, L., Blackburn, S., Borie, M., Caney, S., Chu, E., Edwards, G., Fourie, K., Fraser, A., Heyward, C., Jeans, H., McQuistan, C., Paavola, J., Page, E., Pelling, M., Priest, S., Swiderska, K., Tarazona, M., Thornton, T., Twigg, J., & Venn, A. (2021). An agenda for ethics and justice in adaptation to climate change. *Climate and Development, 13*(1), 1–9. https://doi.org/10.1080/17565529.2019.1700774

Carter, T. R., Benzie, M., Campiglio, E., Carlsen, H., Fronzek, S., Hildén, M., Reyer, C. P. O., & West, C. (2021). A conceptual framework for cross-border impacts of climate change. *Global Environmental Change, 69*, 102307. https://doi.org/10.1016/j.gloenvcha.2021.102307

Carvalho, T. M. N., Niekler, A., Kuhlicke, C., Zscheischler, J., & de Brito, M. M. (2025). *Global synthesis of peer-reviewed articles reveals blind spots in climate impacts research*. Research Square. https://doi.org/10.21203/rs.3.rs-6095740/v1

Centeno, M. A., Nag, M., Patterson, T. S., Shaver, A., & Windawi, A. J. (2015). The emergence of global systemic risk. *Annual Review of Sociology, 41*, 65–85. https://doi.org/10.1146/annurev-soc-073014-112317

Cumiskey, L., Parviainen, J., Bharwani, S., Ng, N., Bagli, S., Drews, M., Genillard, C., Hedderich, D., Hochrainer-Stigler, S., Hofbauer, B., Huszti, L., Kropf, C. M., Löhrlein, J., Pou, A. M., Mazzoli, P., Pedersen, J., Rosa, A., Schweizer, P.-J., Steinhausen, M., et al. (2025). Capacity development for locally-led knowledge co-production processes in Real World Labs for managing climate and disaster risk. *International Journal of Disaster Risk Reduction, 125*, 105398. https://doi.org/10.1016/j.ijdrr.2025.105398

Döll, P., & Romero-Lankao, P. (2017). How to embrace uncertainty in participatory climate change risk management—A roadmap. *Earth's Future, 5*(1), 18–36. https://doi.org/10.1002/2016EF000411

Ducros, G., Tiggeloven, T., Ma, L., Daloz, A. S., Schuhen, N., & de Ruiter, M. C. (2024). Multi-hazards in Scandinavia: Impacts and risks from compound heatwaves, droughts and wildfires. *EGUsphere*, 1–25. https://doi.org/10.5194/egusphere-2024-3158

Fiorino, D. J. (1990). Citizen participation and environmental risk: A survey of institutional mechanisms. *Science, Technology & Human Values, 15*(2), 226–243. https://doi.org/10.1177/016224399001500204

Fischhoff, B. (1995). Risk perception and communication unplugged: Twenty years of process. *Risk Analysis, 15*(2), 137–145. https://doi.org/10.1111/j.1539-6924.1995.tb00308.x

Fisher, E. (2012). Risk and governance. In D. Levi-Faur (Ed.), *The Oxford handbook of governance* (pp. 417–428). Oxford University Press.

Folke, C., Biggs, R., Norström, A., Reyers, B., & Rockström, J. (2016). Social-ecological resilience and biosphere-based sustainability science. *Ecology and Society, 21*(3). https://doi.org/10.5751/ES-08748-210341

Folke, C., Carpenter, S., Walker, B., Scheffer, M., Chapin, T., & Rockström, J. (2010). Resilience thinking: Integrating resilience, adaptability and transformability. *Ecology and Society, 15*(4). https://doi.org/10.5751/ES-03610-150420

Folke, C., Hahn, T., Olsson, P., & Norberg, J. (2005). Adaptive governance of social-ecological systems. *Annual Review of Environment and Resources, 30*(1), 441–473. https://doi.org/10.1146/annurev.energy.30.050504.144511

Forrester, J. W. (1961). *Industrial dynamics*. Pegasus Communications.

Fraccascia, L., Giannoccaro, I., & Albino, V. (2018). Resilience of complex systems: State of the art and directions for future research. *Complexity, 2018*(1), 3421529. https://doi.org/10.1155/2018/3421529

Fraser, N., & Honneth, A. (2003). *Redistribution or recognition? A political-philosophical exchange*. Verso.

Gill, J. C., & Malamud, B. D. (2016). Hazard interactions and interaction networks (cascades) within multi-hazard methodologies. *Earth System Dynamics, 7*(3), 659–679. https://doi.org/10.5194/esd-7-659-2016

Groundstroem, F., & Juhola, S. (2021). Using systems thinking and causal loop diagrams to identify cascading climate change impacts on bioenergy supply systems. *Mitigation and Adaptation Strategies for Global Change, 26*(29). https://doi.org/10.1007/s11027-021-09967-0

Habermas, J. (2004). Discourse ethics. In *Ethics: Contemporary readings*. Routledge.

Hansson, S. (2013). *The ethics of risk: Ethical analysis in an uncertain world*. Springer.

Hayenhjelm, M., & Wolff, J. (2012). The moral problem of risk impositions: A survey of the literature. *European Journal of Philosophy, 20*(S1), E26–E51. https://doi.org/10.1111/j.1468-0378.2011.00482.x

Helbing, D. (2013). Globally networked risks and how to respond. *Nature, 497*(7447), 51–59. https://doi.org/10.1038/nature12047

Heyward, C. (2017). Ethics and climate adaptation. In S. M. Gardiner & A. Thompson (Eds.), *The Oxford handbook of environmental ethics* (pp. 474–486). Oxford University Press. https://doi.org/10.1093/oxfordhb/9780199941339.013.42

Hofbauer, B. (2023). Systemic risks and solar climate engineering research. Integrating technology ethics into the governance of systemic risks. *Journal of Risk Research, 26*(12), 1383–1395. https://doi.org/10.1080/13669877.2023.2288010

Holling, C. S. (1973). Resilience and stability of ecological systems. *Annual Review of Ecology, Evolution, and Systematics, 4*, 1–23. https://doi.org/10.1146/annurev.es.04.110173.000245

Hynes, W., Trump, B., Love, P., & Linkov, I. (2020). Bouncing forward: A resilience approach to dealing with COVID-19 and future systemic shocks. *Environment Systems and Decisions, 40*(2), 174–184. https://doi.org/10.1007/s10669-020-09776-x

Innes, J. E., & Booher, D. E. (2004). Reframing public participation: Strategies for the 21st century. *Planning Theory & Practice, 5*(4), 419–436. https://doi.org/10.1080/1464935042000293170

IPCC Intergovernmental Panel on Climate Change. (2023). *Climate change 2022: Impacts, adaptation and vulnerability*. Contribution of Working Group II to the Sixth Assessment Report of the Intergovernmental Panel on Climate Change [H.-O. Pörtner, D. C. Roberts, M. Tignor, E. S. Poloczanska, K. Mintenbeck, A. Alegría, M. Craig, S. Langsdorf, S. Löschke, V. Möller, A. Okem, & B. Rama (Eds.)]. Cambridge University Press. https://doi.org/10.1017/9781009325844

IRGC International Risk Governance Council. (2005). *An introduction to the IRGC risk governance framework* (pp. 1–24). International Risk Governance Council. Accessed June 25, 2025, from www.irgc.org

IRGC International Risk Governance Council. (2018). *IRGC guidelines for the governance of systemic risks. In systems and organisations in the context of transitions.* Accessed June 25, 2025, from www.irgc.org

Keohane, R. O. (2010). Beyond the tragedy of the commons: A discussion of governing the commons: The evolution of institutions for collective action. *Perspectives on Politics, 8*(2), 577–580. https://doi.org/10.1017/S1537592710000368

Keohane, R. O., & Victor, D. G. (2016). Cooperation and discord in global climate policy. *Nature Climate Change, 6*(6), 570–575. https://doi.org/10.1038/nclimate2937

Klinke, A., & Renn, O. (2012). Adaptive and integrative governance on risk and uncertainty. *Journal of Risk Research, 15*(3), 273–292. https://doi.org/10.1080/13669877.2011.636838

Klinke, A., & Renn, O. (2021). The coming of age of risk governance. *Risk Analysis, 41*(3), 544–557. https://doi.org/10.1111/risa.13383

Kuhlmann, S., Stegmaier, P., & Konrad, K. (2019). The tentative governance of emerging science and technology. A conceptual introduction. *Research Policy, 48*(5), 1091–1097. https://doi.org/10.1016/j.respol.2019.01.006

Lawrence, J., Blackett, P., & Cradock-Henry, N. A. (2020). Cascading climate change impacts and implications. *Climate Risk Management, 29*, 100234. https://doi.org/10.1016/j.crm.2020.100234

Lawrence, M., Homer-Dixon, T., Janzwood, S., Rockstöm, J., Renn, O., & Donges, J. F. (2024). Global polycrisis: The causal mechanisms of crisis entanglement. *Global Sustainability, 7*(e6). https://doi.org/10.1017/sus.2024.1

Levi-Faur, D. (2012). From "Big Government" to "Big Governance". In D. Levi-Faur (Ed.), *The Oxford handbook of governance* (pp. 3–18). Oxford University Press.

Lucas, K. (2022). Theory of Systemic Risks: Insights from Physics and Chemistry. *Risk Analysis, 42*(9), 1935–1944. https://doi.org/10.1111/risa.13558

Mele, C., Pels, J., & Polese, F. (2010). A brief review of systems theories and their managerial applications. *Service Science, 2*(1–2), 126–135. https://doi.org/10.1287/serv.2.1_2.126

Miller, D. (2025). Justice. In E. N. Zalta & U. Nodelman (Eds.), *The Stanford Encyclopedia of Philosophy*. Metaphysics Research Lab, Stanford University. https://plato.stanford.edu/archives/spr2025/entries/justice/

Nalau, J., Torabi, E., Edwards, N., Howes, M., & Morgan, E. (2021). A critical exploration of adaptation heuristics. *Climate Risk Management, 32*, 100292. https://doi.org/10.1016/j.crm.2021.100292

National Research Council. (2008). *Public participation in environmental assessment and decision making.* National Academies Press. https://doi.org/10.17226/12434

Nozick, R. (1974). *Anarchy, state, and utopia*. Basic Books.
Otto, I. M., Donges, J. F., Cremades, R., Bhowmik, A., Hewitt, R. J., Lucht, W., Rockström, J., Allerberger, F., McCaffrey, M., Doe, S. S. P., Lenferna, A., Morán, N., van Vuuren, D. P., & Schellnhuber, H. J. (2020). Social tipping dynamics for stabilizing Earth's climate by 2050. *Proceedings of the National Academy of Sciences, 117*(5), 2354–2365. https://doi.org/10.1073/pnas.1900577117
Parviainen, J., Hochrainer-Stigler, S., Cumiskey, L., Bharwani, S., Schweizer, P.-J., Hofbauer, B., & Cubie, D. (2025). The Risk-Tandem Framework: An iterative framework for combining risk governance and knowledge co-production toward integrated disaster risk management and climate change adaptation. *International Journal of Disaster Risk Reduction, 116*, 105070. https://doi.org/10.1016/j.ijdrr.2024.105070
Pierre, J. (2000). Introduction: Understanding governance. In J. Pierre (Ed.), *Debating governance: Authority, steering, and democracy* (pp. 1–10). Oxford University Press.
Rawls, J. (1999). *A theory of justice. Revised edition*. Belknap Press of Harvard University Press.
Renn, O. (2008). *Risk governance: Coping with uncertainty in a complex world*. Routledge.
Renn, O., & Klinke, A. (2012). Complexity, uncertainty and ambiguity in inclusive risk governance. In *Risk and social theory in environmental management* (pp. 59–76). CSIRO Publishing.
Renn, O., Klinke, A., & van Asselt, M. (2011). Coping with complexity, uncertainty and ambiguity in risk governance: A synthesis. *Ambio, 40*(2), 231–246. https://doi.org/10.1007/s13280-010-0134-0
Renn, O., Laubichler, M., Lucas, K., Kröger, W., Schanze, J., Scholz, R. W., & Schweizer, P.-J. (2022). Systemic risks from different perspectives. *Risk Analysis, 42*(9), 1902–1920. https://doi.org/10.1111/risa.13657
Renn, O., & Schweizer, P.-J. (2009). Inclusive risk governance: Concepts and application to environmental policy making. *Environmental Policy and Governance, 19*(3), 174–185. https://doi.org/10.1002/eet.507
Renn, O., & Schweizer, P.-J. (2020). Inclusive governance for energy policy making: Conceptual foundations, applications, and lessons learned. In O. Renn, F. Ulmer, & A. Deckert (Eds.), *The role of public participation in energy transitions* (pp. 39–79). Academic Press.
Rhodes, R. A. W. (2012). Waves of governance. In S. Levi-Faur (Ed.), *The Oxford handbook of governance* (pp. 33–48). Oxford University Press.
Schröter, K., Schweizer, P.-J., Gräler, B., Cumiskey, L., Bharwani, S., Parviainen, J., Kropf, C. M., Håkansson, V. W., Drews, M., Irvine, T., Dondi, C., Apel, H., Löhrlein, J., Hochrainer-Stigler, S., Bagli, S., Huszti, L., Genillard, C., Unguendoli, S., Hattermann, F., and Steinhausen, M. (2024). Invited perspec-

tives: Fostering interoperability of data, models, communication, and governance for disaster resilience through transdisciplinary knowledge co-production, *Natural Hazards and Earth System Sciences*. https://doi.org/10.5194/nhess-25-3055-2025, 2025.

Schweizer, P.-J. (2021). Systemic risks – Concepts and challenges for risk governance. *Journal of Risk Research, 24*(1), 78–93. https://doi.org/10.1080/13669877.2019.1687574

Schweizer, P.-J., Goble, R., & Renn, O. (2022). Social perception of systemic risks. *Risk Analysis, 42*(7), 1455–1471. https://doi.org/10.1111/risa.13831

Schweizer, P.-J., & Juhola, S. (2024). Navigating systemic risks: Governance of and for systemic risks. *Global Sustainability, 7*, e38. https://doi.org/10.1017/sus.2024.30

Schweizer, P.-J., & Renn, O. (2019). Governance of systemic risks for disaster prevention and mitigation. *Disaster Prevention and Management: An International Journal, 28*(6), 862–874. https://doi.org/10.1108/DPM-09-2019-0282

Sillmann, J., Christensen, I., Hochrainer-Stigler, S., Huang-Lachmann, J.-T., Juhola, S., Kornhuber, K., Mahecha, M. D., Mechler, R., Reichstein, M., Ruane, A. C., Schweizer, P.-J., & Williams, S. (2022). *Briefing note: Systemic risks—Review and opportunities for research, policy and practice from the perspective of climate, environmental and disaster risk science and management.* International Science Council. SC-UNDRR-RISK KAN. https://doi.org/10.24948/2022.01

Slovic, P. (1993). Perceived risk, trust, and democracy. *Risk Analysis, 13*(6), 675–682. https://doi.org/10.1111/j.1539-6924.1993.tb01329.x

Sterman, J. D. (2000). *Business dynamics: Systems thinking and modeling for a complex world.* MacGraw-Hill Company.

Stirling, A. (2006). Analysis, participation and power: Justification and closure in participatory multi-criteria analysis. *Land Use Policy, 23*(1), 95–107.

Taebi, B. (2017). Bridging the gap between social acceptance and ethical acceptability. *Risk Analysis, 37*(10), 1817–1827. https://doi.org/10.1111/risa.12734

Taleb, N. N. (2010). *The Black Swan. The impact of the highly improbable.* Penguin Books.

UNDRR United Nations Office for Disaster Risk Reduction. (2019). *Global assessment report on disaster risk reduction 2019.* United Nations Office of Disaster Risk Reduction. https://www.undrr.org/publication/global-assessment-report-disaster-risk-reduction-2019

UNDRR United Nations Office for Disaster Risk Reduction. (2023). *GAR special report 2023—Mapping resilience for the sustainable development goals.* https://www.undrr.org/gar/gar2023-special-report

UNDRR United Nations Office for Disaster Risk Reduction. (2025). *Global assessment report on disaster risk reduction 2025: Resilience pays: Financing and investing for our future* (1st ed.). United Nations Publications.

Valentini, L. (2012). Ideal vs. non-ideal theory: A conceptual map. *Philosophy Compass, 7*(9), 654–664. https://doi.org/10.1111/j.1747-9991.2012.00500.x

van der Sluijs, J. P., Craye, M., Funtowicz, S., Kloprogge, P., Ravetz, J., & Risbey, J. (2005). Combining quantitative and qualitative measures of uncertainty in model-based environmental assessment: The NUSAP system. *Risk Analysis, 25*(2), 481–492. https://doi.org/10.1111/j.1539-6924.2005.00604.x

Webler, T., & Tuler, S. (2021). Four Decades of Public Participation in Risk Decision Making. *Risk Analysis, 41*(3), 503–518. https://doi.org/10.1111/risa.13250

Whyte, K. P. (2011). The recognition dimensions of environmental justice in Indian country. *Environmental Justice, 4*(4), 199–205. https://doi.org/10.1089/env.2011.0036

Williams, B., & Hummelbrunner, R. (2010). *Systems concepts in action: A practitioner's toolkit.* Stanford University Press.

World Economic Forum. (2024). *Global risks report 2024.* World Economic Forum. https://www.weforum.org/publications/global-risks-report-2024/digest/

Young, I. M. (2011). *Responsibility for justice.* Oxford University Press.

CHAPTER 4

International Climate Change Adaptation Governance: The Evolution of Risk Management Models

Mark Rhinard and Claudia Morsut

Abstract This chapter traces the evolution of risk management models in international climate change adaptation governance, focusing on the United Nations and the European Union. It identifies six generations of risk models, showing how they have shifted from scenario-based assessments to iterative, resilience-based, and transformative frameworks. Risk models have enabled structured, evidence-based adaptation planning, helping policymakers manage uncertainty and allocate resources. Yet, drawing on critical scholarship, the chapter also highlights how these models can obscure political contestation, marginalise justice concerns, and privilege technocratic solutions. While the United Nations and European Union have institutionalised risk governance differently, both now emphasise systemic and transboundary climate risks. As adaptation

M. Rhinard (✉)
Stockholm University, Stockholm, Sweden
e-mail: mark.rhinard@su.se

C. Morsut
University of Stavanger, Stavanger, Norway
e-mail: claudia.morsut@uis.no

C. Morsut (ed.), *Adapting to Climate Change*,
https://doi.org/10.1007/978-3-032-07136-1_4

becomes central to global governance, a seventh generation of risk models may be emerging—one that must reconcile the benefits of risk-based approaches with their limitations. The chapter calls for more pluralistic, reflexive, and justice-aware models to guide adaptation in a world of cascading climate crises.

Keywords Climate change adaptation • European Union • Risk management models • United Nations

4.1 Introduction

Climate change adaptation has been a major international governance challenge over the past three decades. As the impacts of climate change intensify and diversify, policymakers have sought out frameworks to guide adaptation policy in a way that is both responsive to uncertainty and capable of mobilising long-term action. International organisations—particularly the United Nations (UN) and the European Union (EU)—have played key roles in shaping these frameworks. While adaptation governance has taken slightly different institutional forms in these bodies, one common trend has been the increasing reliance on risk assessment models in climate change adaptation governance. These models aim to assess, manage, and reduce the adverse consequences of climate change, and they promise a systematic way to address uncertainty. These models are now deeply embedded in international adaptation approaches, influencing how climate threats are diagnosed, how resources are allocated, and how responsibilities are distributed (Morsut & Rhinard, 2025).

Based on the premise that the kind of risk modelling used in climate change adaptation governance strongly shapes outcomes (Kythreotis et al., 2024), this chapter traces how those risk assessment models have evolved in the past three decades within the UN and the EU. It notes that early, fairly simplistic models based on straightforward scenarios have shifted more recently towards complex, systemic, and broadly participatory risk modelling approaches (Bowyer et al., 2015; Schinko et al., 2024). Understanding this evolution is crucial, not only because it reveals how adaptation challenges are diagnosed and addressed, but also because the choice of modelling frameworks can have important effects on governance outcomes. Risk management models help to clarify threats, structure decision-making, and allocate resources, enabling evidence-based adaptation. Yet they also embed assumptions, prioritise certain risks over others, assume controllability, and can marginalise deeper social, ethical, or political concerns (Boin et al., 2016).

As Jones and Preston (2011) argue, while risk management offers a flexible and widely accepted governance approach, its application to adaptation carries both promise and peril: it can foster learning and institutional alignment, or it can constrain imagination and depoliticise urgent debates. Tracing how these models have evolved thus offers important insights into how climate change is governed in practice. By following the trajectory of risk models, we can see how adaptation governance has been shaped by shifting assumptions about knowledge, control, and responsibility. This chapter examines that trajectory to understand both the institutional innovations and the political implications of governing through risk.

To explore these dynamics, this chapter adopts a historical-analytical approach to trace the evolution of risk assessment models in international adaptation governance. We follow in the footsteps of Jones and Preston (2011), who identified four early generations of climate risk assessment frameworks. We extend the analysis beyond 2011 to capture newer developments in risk assessment modelling, including broader iterative, resilience-based, and transformative approaches. Our focus on risk assessment models stems from earlier research on UN–EU interaction in climate change adaptation governance, conducted as part of the RISKSEC2.0 project. In that study, risk modelling emerged as a recurring but secondary theme in explaining how adaptation strategies are shaped (Morsut & Rhinard, 2025). By identifying successive 'generations' of risk assessment models, we reveal in this chapter how key climate adaptation-related risk assessment models have evolved.

The chapter proceeds in four steps: first, we set out our approach and conceptual lens, drawing on insights from Security Studies, Risk Governance, and the literature on governing through models. Second, we examine the early generations of risk models from the 1990s to 2010. Third, we analyse post-2011 developments, including transboundary and transformative risk approaches. Finally, we compare the institutionalisation of these models in the UN and EU and reflect on the broader implications for future adaptation governance.

4.2 Governing Climate Change Adaptation Through Risk: What Is at Stake?

Risk governance has emerged as the dominant paradigm for managing climate uncertainty, offering structured methodologies for assessing, anticipating, and responding to climate risks (Barquet et al., 2024; Rhinard et al., 2024). In contrast to earlier framings that treated climate change as an existential threat requiring urgent political action, risk-based adaptation presents climate disruption as a manageable challenge (Morsut & Rhinard, 2025). It reframes the problem in technical terms as something that can be quantified, modelled, and addressed through evidence-based interventions. Put differently, the 'riskification' of adaptation policy (Corry, 2012) aligns with a broader transformation in governance that privileges probabilistic reasoning, expert authority, and anticipatory planning over contestation and political choice.

Fundamentally, the logic of risk modelling implies that future harms can be anticipated and mitigated with sufficient knowledge, planning, and institutional coordination. This logic clearly appeals to policymakers at all governance levels because it transforms uncertainty into 'governable terrain'. Risk models help diagnose threats, structure decision-making processes, and allocate resources with the goal of reducing vulnerability. In doing so, they render climate change intelligible and actionable, allowing governments—and international organisations like the UN and EU—to develop adaptation strategies that appear systematic and justifiable.

Yet this core assumption—that climate risks can be carefully managed—is not without criticism, and scholars in the Crisis Management field caution that the promise of risk modelling may be overstated (Boin et al., 2016; McConnell, 2011). Risk governance, they argue, assumes a level of predictability and institutional responsiveness that fails to materialise in practice. Tomorrow's crisis never reflects the exact features of yesterday's crisis, and unthinkable events tend to overwhelm systems, reveal coordination failures, and provoke political contestation rather than a seamless technical response. Thus, risk models may offer a false sense of control, fostering institutional complacency and crowding out more adaptive, learning-oriented approaches to governing uncertainty. In an earlier work, Boin et al. (2006) contend that the very tools meant to anticipate cascading failures often struggle to detect or respond to unexpected developments—a particularly troubling gap in the climate change adaptation domain, as pointed out by several scholars (Kythreotis et al., 2024; Schulz & Siriwardane, 2015).

A second body of scholarship drawing on critical Security Studies (see Chap. 2) raises other issues about the implications of risk-based governance. Generally speaking, scholars in this field contend that the incorporation of risk does not merely enable technical management of uncertainty—it also reshapes the political landscape in subtle but consequential ways. According to this view, risk models function as governing technologies: they do not simply represent reality, but actively construct it (Aradau & van Munster, 2007). By framing climate change as a calculable risk, these models delimit which solutions are seen as viable, which actors are empowered to act, and whose knowledge is perceived as 'legitimate' in the policymaking process (Corry, 2012).

This depoliticising effect is one of the primary concerns of the Security Studies literature, as Chap. 2 has shown. When adaptation is conceptualised primarily as a technical challenge, rather than a political or normative one, important questions around justice, accountability, and distribution may be sidelined (Burke, 2022; Huysmans, 2014). Key questions emerge, such as: Who decides what constitutes an acceptable risk? Whose vulnerabilities are modelled, and whose are overlooked? Which forms of knowledge are treated as legitimate? Scholars warn that a risk-based approach, for all its procedural rationality, can obscure the structural drivers of climate vulnerability and reduce adaptation to a managerial exercise that leaves underlying inequalities intact.

The metaphor of the 'governmentality of unease', developed by Bigo (2006), adds further nuance. In this framework, risk governance, is not about eliminating threats but about managing unease: sustaining a state of low-level alertness through diffuse, everyday mechanisms. In climate change adaptation, risk models perform this function by translating climate volatility into decision matrices and scenario plans. But this translation may come at a cost: as Huysmans (2014) argues, it narrows the scope of legitimate political action and reinforces technocratic authority at the expense of democratic deliberation.

Even within the Risk Governance community (as depicted in Chap. 2), there is growing debate over how risk models should be constructed, applied, and interpreted. Early models were often based on linear projections and isolated hazard assessments and were criticised for their narrowness (Arnall, 2023; Bowyer et al., 2015; Schinko et al., 2024). They tended to privilege environmental data and cost-benefit calculations while overlooking social, institutional, and distributive dimensions of climate vulnerability. These models offered clarity and simplicity, of course—easy to implement—but also masked complexity and uncertainty.

As we will see below, more recent modelling approaches have sought to address these shortcomings. Today's models are broader, often participatory, and explicitly incorporate social, political, and justice-oriented variables. Concepts such as iterative risk management, resilience planning, and transformative adaptation reflect this shift. For instance, the integration of climate justice concerns, systemic risk assessments, and transboundary spillovers marks a significant evolution in both model content and function. These broader models provide a more comprehensive picture of adaptation needs and potential co-benefit, but they also raise new challenges. They may be more difficult to validate, harder to communicate to policymakers, and could generate conflicting priorities across systems.

This expansion of scope reflects a familiar trade-off in governance: between analytical clarity and broader inclusivity (Goodin, 1996). As more variables and actors are incorporated, models can become harder to interpret and apply, potentially leading to a kind of 'complexity paralysis'. This challenge raises the question of whether simpler models that support action are preferable to more complex ones that risk indecision. Understanding the evolution of risk assessment models in climate change adaptation is therefore important, not only to see how approaches have changed, but also to evaluate how well they support effective and equitable governance.

The embeddedness of risk-based approaches in international climate change adaptation governance raises a final question worth addressing: How do certain risk models come to be adopted and why do they subsequently evolve? This chapter builds on recent research that traced how the UN and EU gradually converged on adaptation strategies deeply shaped by risk logics, even though these organisations pursued separate pathways of climate securitisation.[1] Although not the focus of that research, the question of how such risk models emerge, 'travel', and evolve arose in those findings.

[1] Our earlier work (Morsut & Rhinard, 2025) focused on the emergence and interaction of securitising moves, showing how climate change adaptation was increasingly framed in different, securitised ways, and how adaptation policy became infused, at the UN and then the EU, with risk-oriented language, actors, and instruments. However, that study did not unpack the evolution of risk models themselves.

Part of the answer with relevance here lies in the role of expert-based networks that cross the boundaries of academia, policymaking, and international organisations. These networks are often composed of technical specialists, senior civil servants, consultants, and scientists who act as epistemic brokers—advancing specific ways of framing climate risks and promoting preferred methodologies for their assessment and management. The same individuals frequently appear as Intergovernmental Panel on Climate Change (IPCC) lead authors, United Nations Framework Convention on Climate Change (UNFCCC) negotiators, and EU working group members, and act as consultants for national governments, for instance. Through repeated interactions at conferences, technical workshops, expert panels, and report-writing committees, these actors help stabilise certain risk frameworks. Their involvement ensures that particular modelling approaches are seen as credible, methodologically sound, and even politically viable. Over time, these networks establish path dependencies in the governance of climate change adaptation, favouring specific kinds of models that reflect and reinforce prevailing assumptions. While space limitations prevent this chapter from a full analytical tracing of the role of such actors in the evolution of risk models, these background mechanisms are worth reflecting upon and shall be revisited in the conclusion.

In sum, the discussion above outlined the appeal and the limits of risk modelling in climate change adaptation governance and discussed how those models come to be. While risk-based approaches offer structured ways to manage uncertainty, they also face criticism from Crisis Management scholars, and security theorists, and even within the Risk Governance field itself. Such insights contextualise the empirical discussion that follows, which examines how risk models have evolved over the decades, how they have been institutionalised at the UN and EU, and, in the conclusion, what their evolution says about the strengths and limitations of different approaches to governing climate change adaptation.

4.3 The First Generations of Risk Management Models (1990s–2010)

The governance of climate change adaptation has evolved through distinct generations of risk management models, each reflecting different assumptions about how climate risks should be assessed and addressed. From the 1990s to 2010, we can identify three primary generations of risk models that shaped international adaptation policy. The first generation (1990s) was primarily based on scientific impact assessments, where adaptation was framed as a reactive necessity in response to projected climate impacts. The second generation (early 2000s) introduced more structured vulnerability assessments, incorporating social and economic dimensions of climate risk. The third generation (mid- to late 2000s) saw the emergence of early Risk Governance frameworks, marking a shift towards proactive, institutionally embedded adaptation planning (Bowyer et al., 2015; Jones & Preston, 2011).

During these early phases, climate change adaptation governance was highly scenario-driven, focusing on predicting long-term impacts rather than integrating real-time risk governance. The dominant approach to adaptation planning was linear and deterministic—climate models were used to project environmental changes, and adaptation strategies were designed accordingly. This approach was heavily influenced by impact assessment methodologies, which prioritised cost-benefit analyses, hazard mapping, and vulnerability indices to guide decision-making (Jones & Preston, 2011).

4.3.1 First Generation

The *first generation* of adaptation governance models (1990s–early 2000s) was primarily shaped by the IPCC and its successive assessment reports (1990, 1995, 2001). These reports provided scenarios of climate risk and vulnerability, which became the foundation for national and international adaptation planning (Jones & Preston, 2011). During this period, adaptation remained secondary to mitigation in international climate policy. Indeed, the UNFCCC, established in 1992, prioritised emission reductions, while adaptation was viewed as a 'last-resort' measure for vulnerable regions, often in the Global South. However, as climate projections became more precise, adaptation began to gain institutional traction. Early UN climate change adaptation programmes focused on assessing potential climate impacts, largely through downscaled climate models and environmental impact studies.

A turning point came with the Kyoto Protocol (1997), which introduced early financial mechanisms for climate change adaptation, including the Adaptation Fund. It is worth mentioning, though, that this protocol was designed to financially support developing countries in their efforts to reduce the consequences of climate change. Nonetheless, these efforts laid the groundwork for more structured adaptation planning, but early risk models remained focused on environmental hazards rather than integrated governance approaches.

4.3.2 Second Generation

By the early 2000s, climate change adaptation governance began to move beyond static impact assessments to incorporate vulnerability-based approaches, arguably owing to the stronger focus on the needs of developing counties, considered more exposed to climate change impacts. The *second generation* of risk models introduced structured vulnerability assessments, which considered social, economic, and governance factors that influenced climate risk exposure (Jones & Preston, 2011). The UNFCCC's introduction of National Adaptation Programmes of Action (NAPAs) in 2001 was a major institutional development in this period. Designed for least developed countries, NAPAs required governments to identify climate vulnerabilities and prioritise adaptation measures based on systematic assessments. These plans relied heavily on risk assessments, scenario modelling, and cost-effectiveness analysis, reflecting the growing institutionalisation of risk-based adaptation governance. However, NAPAs faced significant limitations, including funding constraints, technical capacity issues, and weak integration into national development strategies (Bowyer et al., 2015; Jones & Preston, 2011).

At the same time, the EU began engaging with climate change adaptation governance, though at a slower pace than the UN. The European Climate Change Programme (2000) included early discussions on adaptation, but adaptation was largely treated as a sectoral issue rather than a standalone governance priority. During this period, the IPCC Third Assessment Report (2001) expanded on risk-based adaptation approaches, recommending multi-criteria decision analysis and structured vulnerability frameworks to guide adaptation planning (Morsut & Rhinard, 2025). This shift reflected a growing recognition that climate adaptation could not be reduced to technical impact assessments alone since it required governance mechanisms to manage uncertainty over time (Jones & Preston, 2011).

4.3.3 Third Generation

What can be called the *third generation* of risk models (mid- to late 2000s) marked a transition towards proactive, institutionally embedded climate change adaptation governance. During this period, risk governance frameworks began to emerge, incorporating resilience-based approaches and structured decision-making tools. At the UN level, the IPCC Fourth Assessment Report (2007) introduced the concept of iterative risk assessment, arguing that adaptation must be an ongoing process rather than a one-time planning exercise. This report reinforced the need for institutional adaptation strategies, paving the way for the 2010 Cancun Adaptation Framework, which further integrated risk governance principles into UN adaptation policy. The EU's 2007 Green Paper on Adapting to Climate Change in Europe—Option for EU Action marked its first major institutional engagement with climate change adaptation governance (European Commission, 2007). While still primarily based on scenario-driven impact assessments, the 2009 White Paper on Adapting to Climate Change: Towards a European Framework for Action (European Commission, 2009) introduced structured risk governance mechanisms, emphasising (a) multi-level governance approaches, involving national, regional, and local adaptation strategies, (b) the need for integrated risk assessments, linking climate risk to broader economic and social policies, and (c) financial mechanisms to support adaptation, such as the European Structural and Investment Funds (Bowyer et al., 2015; Morsut & Rhinard, 2025).

Despite these advancements, early EU climate change adaptation governance remained fragmented, with risk models applied inconsistently across different policy areas. Within the EU, adaptation was still largely treated as an extension of existing environmental management frameworks, rather than a distinct governance challenge requiring systemic institutional coordination.

4.4 Later Generations of Risk Management Models (2011–Present)[2]

The limitations of earlier scenario-driven and vulnerability-based models became increasingly apparent in the early 2010s. Static, long-term projections struggled to accommodate rapidly changing climate dynamics and challenges related to uncertainty, while early adaptation strategies often failed to integrate real-time policy adjustments and multi-level governance mechanisms (Bowyer et al., 2015; Walker et al., 2024).

[2] The authors are grateful for research assistance help from Evelina Jonsson, a PhD student at the Department of Economic History and International Relations at Stockholm University, and for her initial reflections on the evolution of risks management models in the EU and UN.

4.4.1 Fourth Generation

We can identify a *fourth generation* of risk management models emerging after the 2010s. This fourth generation contributed to iterative risk management, adaptive pathways, and flexible decision-making. These three dimensions often overlapped and, in the documents analysed, it is sometimes difficult to distinguish them due to the influence they exert on one another. Their complementarity allowed them to overcome certain limitations of the previous models, for example, to manage uncertainties related to climate change better and to address changes in the climate through more precise calculations. The period after the 2010s represented a transition away from static risk models, as climate change adaptation governance shifted towards dynamic, flexible strategies that could accommodate new climate science, economic constraints, and evolving risk landscapes.

A major milestone during this period was the IPCC's Fifth Assessment Report (IPCC, 2014), which played a decisive role in mainstreaming iterative risk management. While earlier reports, such as the Fourth Assessment Report (IPCC, 2007), acknowledged the utility of iterative approaches, and scholars like Jones and Preston (2011) argued that the IPCC had implicitly promoted iterative thinking from the outset, the Fifth Assessment Report formally institutionalised this logic. It explicitly endorsed 'iterative risk management' as the dominant paradigm for climate change adaptation, integrating it into the broader risk governance framework (IPCC, 2014).

Iterative risk management (also referred to as 'adaptive risk management') is a cyclical and continuous process of identifying, assessing, and mitigating risks. Unlike earlier one-time assessments, this approach assumes that climate risks evolve over time and thus require ongoing reassessment and adjustment. The Fifth Assessment Report positioned iterative risk management as the most suitable way to manage long-term uncertainties, to promote learning, and for allowing flexible decision-making. It laid out a systematic process involving stages of risk identification, implementation, monitoring, and revision, ensuring adaptation strategies could remain responsive to emerging knowledge and shifting vulnerabilities.

This evolution was mirrored within the European Union. We consider the EU's Green Paper on Adapting to Climate Change in Europe – Options for EU Action (European Commission, 2007) the first official and coordinated policy initiative on climate change adaptation. The following year, the European Parliament passed a resolution supporting the Green Paper's approach. The 2007 Green Paper was followed by the 2009 White Paper on Adapting to Climate Change: Towards a European Framework for Action (European Commission, 2009), which offered a more structured framework for EU climate change adaptation governance. This framework stressed the need to reduce uncertainty through improved knowledge bases, with EU-funded research projects tasked with developing models, datasets, prediction tools, and indicators. These efforts aligned closely with the emerging iterative paradigm by promoting continuous learning and refinement of adaptation strategies.

Both the Green and White Papers advocated for improving disaster and crisis management via enhanced risk management tools and contingency planning. Recognising the cross-border nature of climate impacts, ranging from disaster displacement to potential conflict over natural resources, the EU began framing adaptation as a transnational issue (EEA, 2010). These documents also called for mainstreaming adaptation across other policy domains, including water governance, flood risk management, and external action areas such as poverty reduction and the EU's Common Foreign and Security Policy (European Commission, 2007, 2009; Klein et al., 2005).

A more robust commitment emerged in the EU Adaptation Strategy of 2013, which represented a significant advance in structured climate change adaptation governance. The strategy introduced multi-level adaptation planning, fostering coordination between EU institutions, Member States, and local authorities. It also reinforced the knowledge base component, noting gaps left by the IPCC Fifth Assessment Report, particularly regarding regional risk assessments, damage estimates, cost-benefit analyses of adaptation measures, and tools for monitoring and evaluation (European Commission, 2013). An EU-wide risk and vulnerability assessment was proposed to feed into 'integrated threat and risk assessment reports' (Ibid., 2013, p. 3) by 2018, and Horizon 2020 was launched in part to address these gaps.

The strategy also introduced new knowledge-sharing mechanisms, including the European Climate Adaptation Platform (Climate-ADAPT), launched in 2012. This online platform was designed to assist Member States in aligning their National Adaptation Strategies with EU priorities and with global frameworks such as the UNFCCC. The platform promoted the idea of a circular adaptation process, structured around six guidance steps drawn from the 2013 Guidelines on Developing Adaptation Strategies. These included instructions on performing dynamic, revisable risk and vulnerability assessments based on the IPCC Fourth and Fifth Assessment Reports' methodologies and prior EU-EEA research. This circular model aligns closely with the principles of iterative risk management.

Overall, the rise of iterative risk management reflects a growing awareness of the complexity and evolving nature of climate threats. It offered a more flexible and responsive governance model than its predecessors. However, implementation challenges remain: notably the difficulty of maintaining long-term policy continuity and ensuring coordination across institutions and governance levels. These challenges are especially pressing in the context of fragmented policy competencies, varying national capacities, and the time lag between scientific findings and political action.

4.4.2 *Fifth Generation*

The Paris Agreement (2015) marked a turning point in climate change adaptation governance, reinforcing the need for long-term resilience planning and integrated, cross-sectoral risk management. Unlike previous climate agreements, which had primarily emphasised mitigation, the Paris Agreement established adaptation as a core policy objective, requiring governments to develop National Adaptation Plans (NAPs) within a structured, multi-year framework (Bowyer et al., 2015) and on equal footing with mitigation.

Thanks to the Paris Agreement, we argue that we can witness the contours of a *fifth generation* of risk management models, focusing more on resilience based adaptation and integrated risk governance. These approaches aimed to move beyond sector-specific adaptation towards cross-sectoral and transboundary risk governance. As also argued in Chap. 3 of this book, during this time climate risks were increasingly recognised as systemic, affecting infrastructure, food security, migration, and financial stability. As a result, adaptation planning was increasingly embedded within national economic strategies, rather than treated as a discrete environmental policy domain.

Within the European Union, the Horizon 2020 research and innovation programme played a key role in funding integrated adaptation projects. One of the central initiatives was the PLACARD project (PLAtform for Climate Adaptation and Risk reDuction), which ran from 2015 to 2020. PLACARD aimed to bridge the gap between climate change adaptation and disaster risk reduction by 'fostering dialogue, alignment of terminology, shared data use, and collaboration across policy silos' (SEI,

2025, p. 1). In addition to PLACARD, other Horizon 2020 projects such as RESIN (Climate-RESilient Cities and INfrastructures) and BRIGAID (BRIdging the GAp for Innovations in Disaster resilience) promoted multi-scalar risk assessments that accounted for local, national, and regional vulnerabilities. These initiatives supported a shift in risk modelling related to climate change that can be termed a fifth generation.

Another hallmark of this fifth generation was the broadening of stakeholder engagement. Projects increasingly involved businesses, civil society, and local communities, reflecting a growing recognition that adaptation required societal buy-in and behavioural change, not just policy reform. Resilience thus came to be seen not only as a technical or institutional goal but also as a social process involving co-production of knowledge and shared responsibility.

The shift towards resilience-based adaptation represented a deeper institutionalisation of risk governance, ensuring that climate adaptation was not simply a one-off policy goal but an embedded governance function. However, as climate risks became more complex and systemic, the limitations of resilience-based approaches also emerged, leading to calls for a more transformative approach to adaptation governance.

An example is the EU Report on the Implementation of the EU Strategy on Adaptation to Climate Change published in November 2018 (European Commission, 2018). This report highlighted the need for greater diversification and intensification of adaptation compared to the EU's previous strategy and argued that 'Europe is vulnerable to climate change impacts beyond its borders through, for example, trade, international financial flows, migration, and security' (European Commission, 2018, pp. 14–15). It further solidified a new risk approach by calling for the need to support donor countries in relation to adaptation, to update disaster risk assessment methodologies, and to develop and use instruments required to bring the private sector into a more holistic view of risk management.

4.4.3 Sixth Generation

By 2020, climate change adaptation governance was facing an unprecedented scale of climate challenges. Extreme weather events were becoming more frequent and severe, global supply chains were increasingly disrupted by climate-related disasters, and traditional adaptation approaches were struggling to cope with compounding risks. In response, a *sixth generation* of risk management models introduced a transboundary approach to risk assessment and management. Indeed, transboundary risks related to climate change were almost entirely overlooked in the IPCC reports prior to the Sixth Assessment Report, apart from the Fifth Assessment Report's brief references to 'cross-regional phenomena' and the 'cascading effects' of climate change (Burke, 2022; Carter et al., 2021; IPCC, 2014, 2023).

The Sixth Assessment Report voiced strong arguments for a transboundary approach, arguing that incremental adaptation was insufficient in the face of accelerating climate change. Instead, it called for transformative adaptation strategies, which require large-scale shifts in infrastructure, governance, and financial systems to prepare for long-term climate uncertainties. The report also emphasised greater investment in nature-based solutions, moving beyond purely technological adaptation approaches, and the integration of climate adaptation into global financial stability frameworks, recognising that climate risks pose systemic threats to economies (Bowyer et al., 2015).

The EU's 2021 Adaptation Strategy reflected this evolving governance logic (Morsut & Rhinard, 2025). It strengthened regulatory expectations, requiring that adaptation be mainstreamed into public planning and private investment. The strategy also encouraged cross-border cooperation on shared climate risks, particularly in areas such as water management, food systems, and migration. Importantly, it promoted anticipatory adaptation, shifting emphasis towards proactive risk reduction.

The strategy raised the profile of adaptation within the European Green Deal, positioning it as essential for achieving long-term resilience alongside mitigation. This framing was reinforced by Regulation 2021/1119, the 'European Climate Law', which established climate neutrality by 2050 as a legally binding objective and called for coherence between mitigation and adaptation goals (European Commission, 2021). To support implementation, the strategy aimed to improve adaptation modelling and tools, including efforts to refine asset-level modelling, assessments focused on risks to specific infrastructure and economic assets. In 2023, the EU conducted its first EU-wide climate risk assessment, designed to inform disaster risk prevention and better align national efforts with EU priorities (EEA, 2024). Finally, the strategy emphasised improved data access, multi-level coordination, and accelerated action by Member States, building on platforms like Climate-ADAPT to ensure widespread uptake and implementation.

This period marked the most significant transformation in climate change adaptation governance, as institutions increasingly recognised that climate risks are not isolated phenomena but deeply embedded within social and economic systems. At the same time, the growing complexity of cascading and systemic risks increasingly raised new governance challenges, leading to the development of even more sophisticated risk models in recent years, as we discuss in the conclusion of this chapter.

To summarise, since 2011, risk-based climate change adaptation governance has evolved through multiple generations, each reflecting new approaches to managing uncertainty. The fourth generation (2011–2015) introduced iterative risk assessment, the fifth generation (2015–2020) emphasised resilience-based adaptation, and the sixth generation (2020–present) incorporated transformative adaptation strategies. In the conclusion, we discuss the emerging contours of what might be the *seventh generation* of risk models, thus suggesting that adaptation governance may soon move beyond traditional risk frameworks, requiring new ways of conceptualising and governing climate uncertainty.

The next section will compare how the UN and EU have institutionalised these models, analysing the differences and convergences in their adaptation strategies over time.

4.5 The Institutionalisation of UN and EU Risk Management Models

Having traced the evolution of risk management models over successive generations, we now turn to the question of how these models became embedded in institutional practice. While the trajectory of model development has been broadly similar across international organisations, the ways in which these models are institutionalised vary. This section compares how the United Nations and the European Union have integrated the various risk-based approaches outlined above into their respective adaptation governance systems. In doing so, it highlights both divergence, which is rooted in different mandates and governance architectures, and convergence, driven in part by shared expert networks and a growing consensus around the need for transformative adaptation.[3]

As shown above, the UN and the EU both initially approached adaptation governance through climate impact assessments and vulnerability

[3] More details around these dynamics can be found in Morsut and Rhinard (2025).

analyses, reflecting the dominant logic of adaptation planning in the 1990s and early 2000s. The IPCC First and Second Assessment Reports (1990, 1995) established scientific risk modelling and scenario-driven impact assessments as the primary methods for understanding climate vulnerability. These methodologies influenced both early UN adaptation frameworks (such as the NAPAs) and EU adaptation policies that emerged later, including the 2007 Green Paper on Adaptation and the 2009 White Paper on Adaptation. The 2001 IPCC Third Assessment Report introduced the concept of risk-based adaptation, emphasising structured risk assessments rather than purely reactive impact assessments. This report marked the beginning of what might be called institutional riskification, where climate change adaptation governance became increasingly defined by quantifiable risks, cost-benefit analysis, and probability-based decision-making (Morsut & Rhinard, 2025). Both the UN and the EU integrated these principles into their early adaptation efforts, laying the foundation for iterative, evidence-based adaptation planning in the following decades (Bowyer et al., 2015).

However, although both institutions moved towards iterative risk governance and resilience-based adaptation in the 2010s, their approaches diverged due to differences in institutional scope, financial structures, and legal frameworks. The UN's climate change adaptation governance has been globally focused, with a strong emphasis on developing country adaptation needs and the integration of adaptation within the sustainable development agenda. The 2010 Cancun Adaptation Framework institutionalised National Adaptation Plans (NAPs), which became a key mechanism for integrating risk-based adaptation governance into national planning. Additionally, UN adaptation efforts have relied heavily on climate finance mechanisms, such as the Green Climate Fund, to provide support for climate-vulnerable countries. While these initiatives have successfully mobilised international funding, they have faced challenges in implementation, monitoring, and ensuring equitable access to resources.

By contrast, the EU's approach to climate change adaptation has been shaped, quite naturally, by its governance form, and is thus characterised by multi-level governance, regional coordination, and integration with economic policy. The 2013 EU Adaptation Strategy introduced a structured, multi-level approach that encouraged national and local governments to develop adaptation strategies while aligning them with EU-wide climate objectives. The EU has also made significant investments in research and innovation, particularly through programmes such as Horizon 2020, which funded adaptation-related projects like PLACARD (focusing on integrating disaster risk reduction with adaptation) and CASCADES (analysing transboundary climate risks). Unlike the UN, the EU has embedded adaptation planning within economic and trade policy, treating climate resilience as a strategic component of long-term economic stability.

Despite these differences, expert networks have played a crucial role in shaping adaptation governance in both the UN and the EU. Shared securitising moves and risk-based policy frameworks have facilitated the diffusion of risk models across governance levels, leading to convergence in adaptation strategies despite institutional differences (Morsut & Rhinard, 2025). Expert networks, including IPCC scientific panels, UNFCCC technical working groups, and EU-funded research consortia, have influenced how both organisations conceptualise and implement adaptation strategies. The EU's Climate-ADAPT platform, for instance, has served as a critical knowledge-sharing hub, providing adaptation data and policy guidance that aligns with UN frameworks. Similarly, international adaptation finance mechanisms, such as the Green Climate Fund mentioned above, have integrated EU-developed risk assessment methodologies into their project evaluation frameworks.

Perhaps the most interesting point of convergence between the EU and UN relates to the need for transformative adaptation governance. The IPCC Sixth Assessment Report (2021) stressed the need for deep, systemic shifts in adaptation planning, emphasising that incremental adaptation is no longer sufficient in the face of accelerating climate change. This report mirrored the EU's strategic shift, as reflected in the 2021 Adaptation Strategy, which strengthened regulatory adaptation requirements, cross-border cooperation, and economic integration of adaptation efforts (Morsut & Rhinard, 2025), but which also pointed out some shortcomings of technical approaches (Walker et al., 2024). Both institutions have recognised that climate change adaptation is not merely a technical challenge but a governance transformation process requiring the restructuring of economic systems, governance frameworks, and climate finance mechanisms.

4.6 Conclusion

This chapter has examined the evolution of risk management models in international climate change adaptation governance, revealing how they have come to shape not only how climate threats are diagnosed but also how adaptation strategies are formulated, prioritised, and institutionalised. By extending the foundational work of Jones and Preston (2011), we traced six generations of risk models that evolved in response to new understandings of climate risk and changing governance demands. We showed how international organisations—most notably the United Nations and the European Union—progressively moved from early scenario-driven models to more iterative, resilience-based, and transformative frameworks, culminating in recent efforts to address systemic and transboundary risks. Along the way, expert networks and cross-institutional linkages played a pivotal role in embedding and aligning these models across organisations (Morsut & Rhinard, 2025).

Risk models have brought substantial benefits to adaptation governance. They have translated the complexity and uncertainty of climate change into actionable terms. By quantifying risks, projecting scenarios, and identifying priority areas for intervention, these models help structure long-term decision-making and resource allocation. They support efforts to build institutional coherence, align actors across governance levels, and foster international collaboration (Morsut & Rhinard, 2025). They have also encouraged innovation. As Bowyer et al. (2015) argue, risk models generate demand for new data, improved methodologies, and better monitoring tools. In this sense, risk models have served as key governance instruments—they help make what is a complex and abstract challenge of adaptation more tractable and governable (Barquet et al., 2024; Bowyer et al., 2015).

Yet, as discussed in Sect. 4.2, the very qualities that make risk models powerful and seemingly so useful also raise critical questions about their assumptions and effects. The application of risk logics to governance, while offering procedural rationality and managerial clarity, tends to reframe adaptation as a technical problem—one that can be diagnosed and managed through expert tools (Corry, 2012). This framing may obscure the deeper political, ethical, and distributive dimensions of climate vulnerability. As critical security scholars have shown, governing through risk often sidelines questions such as: Whose risks count? Who defines acceptable thresholds of vulnerability? Which knowledges are treated as valid or ignored? (Aradau & van Munster, 2007; Huysmans, 2014) Risk models may render visible some aspects of climate risk while concealing others, particularly those that are difficult to quantify or that challenge dominant power structures, as urgent climate adaptation needs do.

Indeed, as we approach what might be a *seventh generation* of risk models, new tensions are becoming apparent. On one side, there is growing enthusiasm for predictive modelling, real-time analytics, and AI-based early warning systems, which promise more precise and anticipatory forms of governance (Adger et al., 2018). On the other side, there is a rising recognition—especially from justice-oriented and critical scholars—that traditional models fail to account for structural inequalities, historical responsibilities, and the lived experiences of vulnerable communities (Schinko et al., 2024; Walker et al., 2024). These two 'sensibilities' point in very different directions: one towards the further technical refinement of climate change adaptation governance, the other towards a more transformative rethinking of its foundations.

What we see as an emerging tension calls into question whether the risk-based paradigm is still fit for purpose in a world of cascading, systemic, and 'creeping' climate threats (Boin et al., 2021; Burke, 2022; IPCC, 2023). Risk models assume a degree of linearity, stability, and institutional responsiveness that may no longer hold. While recent generations of modelling have broadened in scope, integrating social and economic variables, supporting participatory processes, and accommodating uncertainty, the core logic of risk governance remains intact: that climate threats can be mapped, modelled, and managed (Boin et al., 2016; McConnell, 2011). As the scale and interdependence of risks expand, so too do the cracks in that logic. Some observers now suggest that even the most dynamic risk models may be too narrow, too technocratic, and too apolitical to guide the kinds of deep societal transformations that effective adaptation may require (Chandler, 2014; Schulz & Siriwardane, 2015).

This chapter has raised another normative question. We included in our analysis the extent to which the UN and EU have been organisational incubators of these different risk management models. Their role begs the question: Are the UN and the EU, in relying on risk-based adaptation models, prioritising the right issues? To their credit, both institutions have made adaptation more visible, systematic, and coordinated. Risk models have enabled them to establish strategic plans, monitor progress, and justify investment. But prioritisation through risk frameworks inevitably favours those risks that are easiest to model or that align with institutional preferences (Morsut & Rhinard, 2025; Schinko et al., 2024). The danger is that the most pressing but politically inconvenient vulnerabilities—again, those rooted in inequality, exclusion, or marginalisation—may be sidelined. Moreover, adaptation challenges that defy neat quantification such as questions of social cohesion, intergenerational equity, or transformative change may be ignored altogether.

We therefore return to a central theme from Sect. 4.2: the importance of recognising what is gained and what is lost when governance is mediated through models. Risk models are not neutral tools. They structure how climate change is understood, who is empowered to act, and which interventions are seen as legitimate (Aradau & van Munster, 2007; Bigo, 2006). As these models become more embedded in institutional routines and legal frameworks, their epistemic foundations and political effects deserve greater scrutiny. To rely solely on risk models is to risk narrowing the field of imagination at precisely the moment when adaptation demands more creativity, greater inclusivity, and heightened political engagement.

In sum, risk management models no doubt remain indispensable for governing climate change adaptation. They offer clarity, coordination, and a basis for long-term planning in the face of uncertainty. However, they may also be increasingly insufficient. As climate change adaptation moves to the centre of global governance agendas, the challenge is not just to refine these models but to supplement them with more pluralistic, justice-based, and politically reflective approaches. The expansive and totalising nature of climate risks means that governance must expand to cover values, voices, and visions that shape what adaptation is and in whose interests it is pursued.

References

Adger, W. N., Brown, I., & Surminski, S. (2018). Advances in risk assessment for climate change adaptation policy. *Philosophical Transactions of the Royal Society A: Mathematical, Physical and Engineering Sciences, 376*(2121), 20180106.

Aradau, C., & van Munster, R. (2007). Governing terrorism through risk: Taking precautions, (un)knowing the future. *European Journal of International Relations, 13*(1), 89–115.

Arnall, A. (2023). Climate change and security research: Conflict, securitisation and human agency. *PLOS Climate, 2*(3), e0000072.

Barquet, K., Englund, M., & Rhinard, M. (2024). Climate adaptation in multi-level governance systems: Security, risk, or normal politics? *Risk, Hazards & Crisis in Public Policy, 15*(4), 441–467.

Barquet, K., Morsut, C., Rhinard, M., Englund, M., et al. (2024). Variations of riskification: Climate change adaptation in four European cities. *Risk, Hazards & Crisis in Public Policy, 15*(4), 491–517.

Bigo, D. (2006). Globalized (in)security: The field and the ban-opticon. In D. Bigo & A. Tsoukala (Eds.), *Illiberal practices of liberal regimes: The (in) security games* (pp. 5–49). L'Harmattan.

Boin, A., 't Hart, P., Stern, E., & Sundelius, B. (2006). *The politics of crisis management: Public leadership under pressure*. Cambridge University Press.

Boin, A., 't Hart, P., Stern, E., & Sundelius, B. (2016). *The politics of crisis management: Public leadership under pressure* (2nd ed.). Cambridge University Press.

Boin, A., Ekengren, M., & Rhinard, M. (2021). Understanding creeping crises: Revisiting the puzzle. In R. A. Boin, M. Ekengren, & M. Rhinard (Eds.), *Understanding the creeping crisis* (pp. 165–177). Palgrave.

Bowyer, P., Schaller, M., Bender, S., & Jacob, D. (2015). Adaptation as climate risk management: Methods and approaches. In W. Leal Filho (Ed.), *Handbook of climate change adaptation* (pp. 71–90). Springer.

Burke, A. D. (2022). An architecture for a net zero world: Global climate governance beyond the epoch of failure. *Global Policy, 13*(3), 68–80.

Carter, T. R., Elsawah, S., et al. (2021). A conceptual framework for understanding the transboundary climate risks of adaptation. *Nature Climate Change, 11*(7), 581–589.

Chandler, D. (2014). *Resilience: The governance of complexity*. Routledge.

Corry, O. (2012). Securitisation and 'riskification': Second-order security and the politics of climate change. *Millennium: Journal of International Studies, 40*(2), 235–258. https://doi.org/10.1177/0305829811419444

EEA European Environment Agency. (2010). *Europe adapts to climate change: Comparing national adaptation strategies*. EEA report no 2/2010.

EEA European Environment Agency. (2024). *European climate risk assessment 2024*. Publications Office of the European Union.

European Commission. (2007). *Green paper: Adapting to climate change in Europe – Options for EU action*. COM(2007)354 final.

European Commission. (2009). *White paper: Adapting to climate change – Towards a European framework for action*. COM(2009)147 final.

European Commission. (2013). *An EU strategy on adaptation to climate change*. COM(2013)216 final.

European Commission. (2018). *Report on the implementation of the EU strategy on adaptation to climate change*. SWD(2018)460 final.

European Commission. (2021). *Regulation (EU) 2021/1119 establishing the framework for achieving climate neutrality (European Climate Law)*.

Goodin, R. E. (1996). Institutions and their design. In R. E. Goodin (Ed.), *The theory of institutional design* (pp. 1–53). Cambridge University Press.

Huysmans, J. (2014). *Security unbound: Enacting democratic limits*. Routledge.

IPCC Intergovernmental Panel on Climate Change. (1990). *Climate change: The IPCC impacts assessment*. Report prepared for Intergovernmental Panel on Climate Change by Working Group II. Australian Government Publishing Service.

IPCC Intergovernmental Panel on Climate Change. (1995). *Impacts, adaptations and mitigation of climate change: Scientific-technical analyses*. Contribution of

Working Group II to the Second Assessment Report of the Intergovernmental Panel on Climate Change. Cambridge University Press.

IPCC Intergovernmental Panel on Climate Change. (2001). *Climate change 2001 working group II: Impacts, adaptation and vulnerability*. Cambridge University Press.

IPCC Intergovernmental Panel on Climate Change. (2007). *Contribution of working group II to the fourth assessment report of the intergovernmental panel on climate change*. Cambridge University Press.

IPCC Intergovernmental Panel on Climate Change. (2014). *Climate change 2014: Impacts, adaptation, and vulnerability*. Contribution of Working Group II to the Fifth Assessment Report of the Intergovernmental Panel on Climate Change. IPCC.

IPCC Intergovernmental Panel on Climate Change. (2023). *Climate change 2022: Impacts, adaptation and vulnerability*. Contribution of Working Group II to the Sixth Assessment Report of the Intergovernmental Panel on Climate Change [H.-O. Pörtner, D. C. Roberts, M. Tignor, E. S. Poloczanska, K. Mintenbeck, A. Alegría, M. Craig, S. Langsdorf, S. Löschke, V. Möller, A. Okem & B. Rama (Eds.)]. Cambridge University Press. https://doi.org/10.1017/9781009325844

Jones, R. N., & Preston, B. L. (2011). Adaptation and risk management. *WIREs Climate Change, 2*(2), 296–308.

Klein, R. J. T., Schipper, E. L. F., & Dessai, S. (2005). Integrating mitigation and adaptation into climate and development policy: Three research questions. *Environmental Science & Policy, 8*(6), 579–588.

Kythreotis, A. P., Hannaford, M., Howarth, C., James, P., Walker, G., & Rayner, T. (2024). Translating climate risk assessments into more effective adaptation decision-making: The importance of social and political aspects of place-based climate risk. *Environmental Science & Policy, 154*, 103705.

McConnell, A. (2011). Success? Failure? Something in-between? A framework for evaluating crisis management. *Policy and Society, 30*(2), 63–76.

Morsut, C., & Rhinard, M. (2025). The collective securitisation of climate change: Implications for adaptation policy in the European Union and United Nations. *Review of International Studies*, 1–26. https://doi.org/10.1017/S0260210525100867

Rhinard, M., et al. (2024). Understanding variation in national climate change adaptation: Securitization in focus. *Environment and Planning C, 42*(4), 676–696.

Schinko, T., Karabaczek, V., Menk, L., & Kienberger, S. (2024). Identifying constraints and limits to climate change adaptation in Austria under deep uncertainty. *Frontiers in Climate, 6*, 1303767.

Schulz, K., & Siriwardane, R. (2015). *Depoliticised and technocratic? Normativity and the politics of transformative adaptation* (Earth system governance working paper no. 33). Earth System Governance Project.

SEI. (2025). *Stockholm Environmental Institute*. Accessed June 13, 2025, from PLACARD HUB website, www.sei.org/projects/placard/#the-placard-connectivity-hub

Walker, S. E., Smith, E. A., Bennett, N., Bannister, E., Narayana, A., Nuckols, T., Pineda Vélez, K., Wrigley, J., & Bailey, K. M. (2024). Defining and conceptualizing equity and justice in climate adaptation: A scoping review. *Global Environmental Change, 87*, 102885.

CHAPTER 5

Legitimation of Climate Change Adaptation Policies in Norway: Intersections Between Societal Planning, Technological-Administrative, and Societal Security Discourses

Simon Neby, Ole Andreas Engen, Claudia Morsut, and Elisabeth Angell

Abstract This chapter deepens the relevance of understanding the role of legitimation for developing climate change adaptation policies, on the basis of the discourses that characterise the Norwegian climate change adaptation field. We argue that to understand how policy choices are constructed,

S. Neby (✉)
University of Bergen, Bergen, Norway
e-mail: simon.neby@uib.no

O. A. Engen • C. Morsut
University of Stavanger, Stavanger, Norway
e-mail: ole.a.engen@uis.no; claudia.morsut@uis.no

E. Angell
NORCE Bergen, Bergen, Norway
e-mail: elan@norceresearch.no

C. Morsut (ed.), *Adapting to Climate Change*,
https://doi.org/10.1007/978-3-032-07136-1_5

it is necessary to include a perspective on legitimation. Sound policymaking is not only about creating governance capacity, but also about generating governance legitimacy. Legitimation efforts, therefore, can take different directions. We conclude that legitimation efforts regarding climate change adaptation in Norway are inherently complex matters, reflecting the realities of governance as much as the realities of climate impacts.

Keywords Climate change adaptation • Discourses • Legitimation • Societal planning • Societal safety and security

5.1 Introduction

Climate change adaptation is a policy area that includes anticipating and reacting to both immediate adverse events and long-term climatic impacts. Integral to climate adaptation as a more specific sub-field of climate policy, risk governance and risk management are important parts of public authorities' handling of the climate crisis. In relation to crisis management, the intricate connections between governance capacity and governance legitimacy have received significant attention (see, e.g., Christensen et al., 2016, 2019). Policy choices need justification through reasoning and discourse (Dunn, 1990), which necessitates asking how authorities seek to legitimise their decisions and from where the establishment of capacity draws its legitimacy. This challenge directs attention to *how* public actors approach the issue of legitimation regarding climate change adaptation. As a response to the climate crisis, we would expect adaptation policies to be grounded in concerns of capacity and necessity, utility, and urgency. As part of long-term governance, however, a series of other legitimation rationales may come into play, such as concerns for normative alignments, procedures for decision-making, the use of knowledge, or the political context for discussing adaptation policies.

In this chapter, we discuss legitimation strategies identifiable in Norwegian discourses about climate change adaptation governance, departing from field-level discourses across levels of governance. Analysing discourses is a powerful tool to unveil such strategies since adaptation governance is expressed in extended arguments and practices regarding policy choices, regulatory and measurament approaches, collective efforts, use of knowledge, and the involvement of actors who address problems and find solutions. Within three interconnected discourses, we uncover the rationale for the legitimation of climate change adaptation policies based on the nature of explicit, implicit, and emerging arguments. Subsequently, we identify different lines of argumentation concerning legitimation strategies about adaptation in Norway. We show that whereas riskification (see introduction in this book) adequately describes the orientation of Norwegian climate change adaptation governance, it is also an approach that is useful for understanding the legitimation strategies public actors engage in, in this small, well-functioning country experiencing climate impacts where societal security and rigid statutory governance are hallmarks.

The context for Norwegian adaptation policies is twofold: on the one hand, it is a policy area that necessarily deals with the nature–society interface where climate change plays out through impacts such as a general increase in—and more intense—precipitation, higher temperatures, melting of permafrost, unseasonal variations in temperature, floods, sea-level rise, drought, landslides, and more (see, e.g., Hanssen-Bauer et al., 2017; Meld. St. 26 (2022–2023), 2023). The local and regional manifestations of these developments are important, and extreme weather events receive significant attention amongst politicians, citizens, and the media. Critical examples are the 2005 Hatlestad landslide in Bergen, the unseasonal 2014 floods in western Norway, and the 2023 floods and landslides occurring during the major weather event Hans (see Chap. 6). Typically, issues such as forecasting, precautionary measures, knowledge application, and crisis management rise to the fore of the political agenda following such events.

On the other hand, Norwegian climate change adaptation governance plays out within the jurisdiction of a highly institutionalised, well-functioning multi-level system (Orderud & Naustdalslid, 2019). Climate change adaptation has previously been dubbed an immature policy field—or the 'lesser brother of climate policies'—and has been sometimes downplayed in terms of importance and salience (Dannevig et al., 2013; Neby et al., 2023a). In recent years, however, central-level Norwegian adaptation policies have emerged as more visible and explicit. This development was modestly signalled with the 2013 White Paper (Meld. St. 33 (2012–2013), 2013) and significantly expanded with the 2023 White Paper (Meld. St. 26 (2022–2023), 2023) on the Norwegian climate policy. Both policy documents signal a move towards a more proactive centralised approach to climate change adaptation, albeit less so in terms of financial prioritisation, resource allocation, and coordination (see Chap. 6). Where aims and suggestions are now more plentiful, detailed, and developed, Norwegian adaptation budgets remain relatively scarce.

Underlining a historical orientation that in terms of governance is distinctly focused on the local level (see Chap. 6), Norwegian climate change adaptation is firmly embedded in existing risk management approaches, where a main tool is statutory risk and vulnerability assessments used to identify climate risks and natural hazards (Lie et al., 2024; Neby et al., 2023b). These assessments are organised as a municipal responsibility through planning legislation and supported by a general framework of public organisations at different levels and of distinct types (regulatory agencies, county governors, knowledge providers). Societal planning comes with a strong focus on regulatory technicalities and a deliberate connection between local political ambitions regarding societal development and the role of planning, underlining principles of democratic autonomy at the municipal level.

Thus, although there is a vertical aspect from the national to the local level in Norwegian climate change adaptation (Westskog et al., 2017), the fact that most relevant climate impacts in Norway have local manifestations, combined with local democratic principles, has led adaptation to become the domain of the municipalities (Karlson et al., 2023; Neby et al., 2023b). As municipalities have explicit, statutory responsibilities for local aspects of societal security based on the Civil Protection Act, an event-driven focus on climate impacts also leads the discourse towards emergency preparedness and safety. Issues of societal security and safety, in contrast to adaptation, receive considerable attention in national political debates, opening a space for climate change adaptation to be interpreted within a safety and preparedness interpretative framework.

Risk governance approaches and risk management tools are central building blocks of Norwegian climate adaptation policies. Most notably, the use of risk assessment tools is not only widespread, but it is also regulated in statutory approaches to planning and preparedness. This situation leads policies, decisions, and measures in technocratically oriented directions and straddles preparedness, planning, and climate-specific issues (Morsut et al., 2024; Neby et al., 2023a). For climate change adaptation, the narrative of an unprecedented crisis is downplayed through the employment of risk governance approaches, which in turn leads climate change adaptation in the direction of *business as usual*. This framing places adaptation within a risk reduction framework that focuses on apolitical statutory issues and rather technical analytical exercises.

Hence, there are several discourses to consider when attempting to uncover the legitimising strategies concerning Norwegian climate change adaptation. One discourse connects to the local level, where spatial planning and societal development, climate impacts, and statutory governance intersect. Secondly, concerning how adaptation practices play out, there is a techno-administrative discourse that focuses on what climate impacts are and how they can be handled through risk management approaches. Thirdly, there is a larger discussion about societal security and safety that cuts across the adaptation issue at all levels of governance.

In what follows, we assess these discourses, outlining their focus and content as observed in our studies, before ending the chapter with a short discussion of our findings and their implications.

5.2 Legitimation Strategies for Climate Change Adaptation

Assessing EU policies for climate change adaptation, Remling (2018) argues that adaptation policy discourses tend to depoliticise the choices made for dealing with climate impacts, often presenting adaptation as a technical and non-political issue. This relates to the framing of heuristics within, and narratives regarding, climate change adaptation policies. The notion of a climate crisis drives a need to understand whether the crisis narrative is significant across levels of governance and to identify the possible implications for legitimate democratic governance in this field. In climate change adaptation, the boundaries between crisis management, disaster preparedness, and societal security are often blurred (see, e.g., Booth et al., 2020; Neby, 2019). The implication is that climate change adaptation navigates both small-scale, localised technical issues and large-scale, society-wide threats.

One analytical approach often used to describe such a situation is *riskification* (Diez et al., 2016; Rhinard et al., 2024). The main characteristic of *riskification* is a focus on the negative potential of possible risks. The approach is oriented towards future scenarios to be handled through risk governance and risk management techniques. Maintaining instrumental elements, riskified approaches signal adaptation as a continuous effort to reduce vulnerabilities through the application of knowledge and statutory, standardised procedures. The relational aspects of governance are reflected in risk management discourses as attention shifts from solving a critical and present problem to *handling it over time* through reliable governance processes. Thus, the focus is mainly on the quality of governance in terms of process and analytical capacity, with adaptation-specific considerations of what 'good governance' is (Schmidt & Wood, 2019; Van Buuren et al., 2014).

Ideas of good adaptation governance reflect issues of legitimacy and legitimation, which are dealt with in different ways in the relevant literature. Dellmuth and Gustafsson (2023) maintain that as policies increasingly coexist across governance levels and geographical scales, the relative distance between national approaches and more specific, local measures increases. Climate change adaptation thus challenges institutional contexts, decision-making, and power relationships, as it is physically linked to local settings but politically part of national and international frameworks. This institutional challenge of vertical and horizontal complexity generates questions of legitimacy (see, e.g., Klein et al., 2016; Mees et al., 2012; Wejs et al., 2014) that connect to both structural issues of the governance apparatus, and to the complex nature of the challenge.

Other studies of adaptation and legitimacy focus on how legitimation strategies are important for the 'mainstreaming' of climate adaptation policies (van Buuren et al., 2014), drawing attention to their discursive aspects. For example, Sygna et al. (2013) show how interpretations of vulnerability can be framed in different ways, focusing on the distinction between a scientific framing and a human security framing. Few et al. (2007) argue that there is an inherent tension between principles of participatory inclusion and anticipatory adaptation, pointing to relationships not only between policymakers and policy takers, but between different spheres of stakeholders and policy agents. Van Buuren et al. (2014) reveal how issues of legitimacy depend on perspective: from a legal perspective, legitimacy becomes a matter of *good governance*; from a planning perspective, it becomes a matter of flexibility, learning, and capacity; whereas from a network perspective, it is a matter of dialogue, involvement, and support. Dellmuth and Gustafsson (2023) argue that climate justice perspectives are as important for legitimacy in adaptation governance as they are for mitigation policies, echoing an argument that climate change adaptation is as political as greenhouse gas reduction, partly because of a need for transformative adaptation (Eriksen et al., 2015).

In the admittedly less adaptation-oriented literature on governance capacity and governance legitimacy, capacity and legitimacy are understood as co-dependent concerns (Christensen & Lægreid, 2020; Lodge & Wegrich, 2014). Legitimacy relies on at least two different tiers: one is about the trust in and perceptions of ideas, measurement approaches, and actors from the surroundings (e.g. the expectation and attitudes amongst citizens towards public office), whereas the other quite differently is connected to arguments of efficiency (e.g. whether authorities are able to achieve their policy aims, how they plan to do so, resource use, and so on). Suchman (1995, p. 572) points to a distinction between strategic and institutional approaches to understanding legitimacy. The former revolves around actors' instrumental efforts to generate support for their choices, whereas the latter studies how sector-wide normative pressures transcend the reach and actions of single actors. The strategic approach relates to how the involved actors justify their policies and practices. However, this cannot be done without consideration of the institutional context: strategies are directed towards the institutional surroundings.

Based on an assessment of policy studies, Shanahan et al. (2013) argue that meaning-making—the process of constructing policy realities—is understudied. This view directs attention towards the narrative and discursive aspect of legitimacy: what the stories told are, and what our interpretations of these stories have to say about how legitimacy is achieved and perceived. In this chapter, we suggest that legitimation strategies may be both instrumental and deliberate, normatively guided, or less calculated. Arguably, strategic legitimacy is about *creating* and *enacting* the acceptance of political and administrative choices, building on the assumption that legitimacy connects to the narrative and language, scenarios and arguments, actions and attitudes *de facto* forwarded by relevant actors (Lund-Tønnesen, 2025).

These notions imply that creating legitimacy reflects different aspects of governance. Hence, we maintain a distinction between the *direction* and the *content* of legitimation. Regarding the former, Scharpf (1999) distinguishes between an *input* and an *output* side of legitimacy. Different factors of legitimacy come into play at different stages of political-administrative processes: legitimacy may stem from *ex ante* perceptions and trust in the system, but also depends on the decisions taken and measures introduced, as well as their *ex post* evaluation. In addition, the notion of *throughput* legitimacy (see, e.g., Schmidt & Wood, 2019) focuses on procedural criteria concerned with the quality of governance. Thus, legitimacy in some respects precedes policy, but it is also created as policies find their form and implementation, and finally, it depends on policy results and the accountability mechanisms that accompany evaluation efforts. These distinctions thus tell us something about the direction the generative approach to legitimacy may take: Is legitimacy connected to the foundations of policymaking, to the policymaking process, or to the effects produced by it?

Quite differently, regarding the substantial content of legitimation efforts, Suchman (1995) distinguishes between *pragmatic, moral, and cognitive* dimensions as a basis for understanding discursive constructions of legitimacy. All three dimensions can be studied by examining the considerations taken within the public apparatus, whether these are based on internal needs or responses to exogenous forces. The pragmatic approach to legitimacy, firstly, concerns the instrumental value and utility of measures and technologies (Suchman, 1995, p. 578), and connects to issues of capacity: the ability to exert effective problem-solving of technical merit. The question of regulation becomes a frame of reference for maintaining the instrumental legitimacy of an existing order. Secondly, moral legitimacy resonates with normativity, in the sense that such strategies are conducted with reference to appropriateness: values and norms that are socially acceptable and appeal to altruistic motives (Suchman, 1995, p. 579). On the one hand, this may suggest that established standards leading to the common good are followed. On the other hand, it suggests the application of expertise and knowledge. Thirdly, there is the idea of cognitive legitimacy, which refers to the strategic framing of which solutions are conceivable and inevitable, and which are not (Lund-Tønnesen, 2025, p. 383). The introduction of new measures in this context revolves around the discursive construction of a particular approach as being the only one imaginable, which in turn renders other alternatives as unimaginable (Ibid.).

Taking both Scharpf (1999) and Suchman (1995) into account, understanding strategic legitimation efforts clearly depends on what part of the policy process we focus on (preconditional input, procedural throughput, efficiency-oriented output), but equally so on the nature of the discursive arguments used (pragmatic, moral, cognitive). Legitimacy is thus inherently contextual—it involves some assessment of *the appropriate.* As Suchman defines it, legitimacy '…is a generalized perception or assumption that the actions of an entity are desirable, proper, or appropriate within some socially constructed system of norms, values, beliefs and definitions' (1995, p. 574).

Analysing the strategic legitimation of climate change adaptation policies, thus, is a matter of analysing the manifest ideas of and arguments about what good climate change adaptation governance is suggested to be. The above understandings of strategic legitimation (i.e. Scharpf,

1999; Suchman, 1995) can be set within the context of riskification and used for this purpose. Next, we turn our focus towards the discursive aspects of Norwegian climate change adaptation, applying the six categories that concern legitimacy as outlined above. In terms of the relative position and direction of legitimacy claims, are they handled as concerns of the input, throughput, or output side of politics? In terms of their relative content, do the relevant discourses reflect a pragmatic, moral, or cognitive orientation? We assess three interconnected—yet distinctly identifiable—discourses: firstly, we dive into municipal planning and statutory governance; secondly, we discuss the techno-administrative discourse on climate adaptation; thirdly, the societal safety and security discourse is assessed.

5.3 Municipal Planning and Statutory Governance

Norwegian climate change adaptation is often localised, place-specific, and organised as a municipal responsibility. A hierarchical delegation is systematically applied through planning regulations that provide standardised requirements and advice. There is also a bottom-up dimension, however, as local governments adjust and adapt to their geographical and physical, organisational, and societal needs (Westskog et al., 2017). Municipal planning is the foremost tool for climate change adaptation at the local level in Norway. The procedures and standards for such planning are subject to law and regulation, but the municipalities themselves are tasked with planning. As opposed to the relative 'fuzziness' of climate-related decision-making (Lempert et al., 2004), planning regulations delineate municipal responsibilities relatively clearly (see Chap. 6).

However, this seemingly clear-cut delineation of responsibility does not mean planning and adaptation are straightforward issues. The utilisation and management of land significantly influence the capacity to address, adapt to, and prevent various climate-related events. Planning directly influences how citizens and businesses can use properties and land, signalling forceful local political priorities. Statutory planning is effectively a general exercise of national political ambitions towards local communities, but it is equally an exercise of local policies towards individuals, businesses, and property owners. Through the direct coupling of spatial adaptation concerns, regulatory tools, and political ambition, both societal and land-use planning are central to preventing undesirable outcomes of climate impacts. For instance, technical limitations for developments, such as distance from waterways or possible landslide paths, transform from knowledge-based assessments into formal regulation. Put differently, plans become the basis for administrative and political decisions about the who, where, what, and why of physical investments in property and infrastructure.

In Norway, municipalities bear the primary responsibility for planning, as mandated by the Planning and Building Act. Its purpose (according to §1) is to promote sustainable development for the benefit of individuals, society, and future generations. A part of that is a coordinative function, as planning according to the law must take national, regional, and local tasks into account across more sector-specific concerns. The act emphasises broad and integrated considerations, including climate concerns and the promotion of societal security. It functions as a procedural law, ensuring transparency, consultation, and participation among affected stakeholders. Residents, organisations, and various interest groups are entitled to provide input on plans under development. State authorities are also involved in municipal planning processes; if national or significant regional interests are inadequately addressed, regional and national authorities may raise objections, preventing plan adoption until disagreements are resolved. Most objections are settled amicably, often leading municipalities to revise their plans accordingly.

A functioning statutory planning process not only produces plans that adhere to judicial standards, but it also ensures that plans are enacted and followed. This process aligns with several of Scharpf's (1999) distinctions: firstly, regarding *input legitimacy*, points of view are emphasised before political decisions are made. There is a degree of representation within these requirements: plans are decided upon by elected politicians, and relevant actors are consulted through the process. The distinction of *throughput legitimacy*, secondly, becomes blurred if we emphasise the procedural aspect of the regulations. Arguably, the procedural orientation of the regulations mainly influences the process of making land-use decisions, with leeway for political prioritisation at the local level. A critical question is thus whether municipalities possess the necessary capacity and expertise to balance the myriad of considerations inherent in planning. Thirdly, this concern extends to whether the final plan achieves what Scharpf (1999) terms *output legitimacy*, by contributing to desired results and end-states. The frequency and nature of stakeholders seeking and obtaining exemptions from land-use plans can serve as indicators of a plan's output legitimacy.

Local land-use planning includes requirements to assess landslide and flood hazards before developing a geographic area (as required by, e.g., the Planning and Building Act § 4-3 and § 11-8). Such issues tend to be depoliticised, treated more as technical and non-political issues (Remling, 2018), often navigated by the use of mandatory risk and vulnerability analyses. Integrating climate change adaptation and societal security into planning shifts the focus towards prevention and aligns with standard, often long-term, processes where multiple societal interests are balanced. This approach contrasts with crisis-oriented strategies. In this context, climate change adaptation becomes one of many considerations within the realm of *business as usual* (Neby et al., 2023a). The result is that determining which interests take precedence in planning processes becomes a normative and political question for local elected politicians. Within the planning field, some aspects of climate adaptation are likely to be treated as part of normal politics, while others are addressed as technical and non-political issues.

That said, municipal planning through statutory frameworks is perhaps the central interface between politics and implementation at the local level, together with financial priorities. Municipal planning allows local governments to prioritise inherently normative issues, such as how land can be set aside for different types of businesses or agriculture, which areas are to be developed for housing, what restrictions should apply, and opportunities to be exploited for societal development in general. These considerations rest well within normative frameworks and perceptions of what a town or city *should be*, extending the range of planning well into the political realm as much as in the direction of pragmatic problem-solving.

5.4 Techno-Administrative Climate Change Adaptation

The climate change adaptation narrative in Norway downplays the unprecedented crisis related to climate change and employs a risk management language, which is mirrored in climate change adaptation measures and practices as well (Morsut et al., 2024; Neby et al., 2023b), especially at the local level. For instance, water-related issues regarding the built environment are important and are often followed up by specialised departments or units based on engineering approaches (Kvamsås, 2022). Such a framing places climate change adaptation within a risk reduction framework that focuses on technical analytical exercises.

As stated above, the Norwegian national authorities have placed the responsibility for climate change adaptation as a response to climate change and its effects at the municipal level. Municipalities are legitimised to handle climate change impacts via adaptation measures and actions following a principle of proximity. For example, the detailed handling of runoffs and spillwater due to increased precipitation becomes a non-political, professional task. This perspective reflects how climate risks are both spatially limited events and concerns of long-lasting complex challenges that relate to a dynamic climate. Such concerns are specific and spatially restricted, e.g. the placement and dimensions of drainage pipes or the re-opening of natural waterways. These technicalities in part manifest in regulatory frameworks (as indicated above), but they also extend to the use of different types of knowledge. For example, hydrological projections and modelling are an integral part of estimating where it is safe to build. Such calculations are typically provided by national-level agencies, research institutions, or consultants and translated into technically detailed maps used for planning purposes. Subsequently, these maps become authoritative, detailing allowances and prohibitions, zones, and areas of particular concern. Some municipalities cooperate with knowledge producers and researchers to generate the necessary analytical capacity, either as part of research project participation or as part of standing, less formalised collaborations. Such cooperation is more commonly found with larger cities, however, indicating that capacity is in part a matter of size.

National authorities promote climate risk management as a relevant tool in adaptation work, especially at the local level (see Chap. 6). Climate risk management approaches were promoted by the Climate Risk Committee's Official Norwegian Report on Climate Risk and the Norwegian Economy (NOU 2018:18, 2018). The committee pointed out that the public sector's exposure to risk has different characteristics from that of the private sector. For example, when considering how climate change impacts society versus the Norwegian economy, the committee argued that there is a gap between macroeconomic foci and the more concrete risk and vulnerability analyses performed by Norwegian municipalities. Most municipalities in Norway have considered climate risk in their risk and vulnerability analyses since then (Rød et al., 2025), mainly as part of their planning procedures. However, including climate risk in existing analyses raises the question of whether the same climate risk will continue to be relevant over time or if new tools and calculations are needed due to the uncertainty concerning climate change. While climate risks are often considered in planning, the implementation of actual adaptation measures is much less widespread (Rød et al., 2025).

Furthermore, adaptation measures are often risk management-driven within existing frameworks, models, and structures that often prescribe active strategies and tools to uncover, analyse, and evaluate climate risk, and determine the level of acceptance and uncertainty. To do so properly requires knowledge of the different risk typologies in general and about climate risks in particular. The statutory framework creates a situation where the question seems to be whether one has planned for adaptation rather than implemented it. That is, as risk and vulnerability analyses are mandatory (including many issues other than climate risks), the administrative use of these analyses is more common than the actual follow-up work to mitigate the potential risks, vulnerabilities, and consequences uncovered. Following templates created by national actors such as the Directorate for Civil Protection (DSB, 2022), the modus operandi typically involves considering the risk rather than finding and introducing measures to mitigate it. The very construction of the risk and vulnerability analyses shapes and guides the content of climate change adaptation work, effectively framing it as risk. The connection between risk and adaptation thus follows an institutionalised approach that penetrates the system. As the risk and vulnerability analyses are both part of statutory requirements, they demand specific knowledge and competencies, and they guide practices.

Regarding the legitimation practices within these aspects of Norwegian climate change adaptation, there are two important things to consider. Firstly, demands for municipal action are nationally warranted, and the statutory arrangements framing the more technical-administrative approaches are more procedural than substantial. Thus, a pragmatic solution for dealing with adaptation is well placed within analyses and risk and vulnerability analyses. The pragmatic aspect is less about *doing adaptation* and more about defining risks, vulnerabilities, and consequences. Secondly, procedure and regulation are important. The notion of a throughput orientation is clear, as the emphasis relies on process requirements over actual results or outcomes. This situation is marked by a potential tension between finding the practical solution to handling procedural demands and using the procedures for outlining pragmatic approaches to the *de facto* implementation of climate change adaptation measures. This part of the Norwegian adaptation work leaves little room for influence by citizens, and the contents produced build on specific methods and procedures. The normativity of the risk and vulnerability approach is thus authoritative, suggesting a strong belief in standardised procedures and a strong risk-based analytical logic.

5.5 Societal Safety and Security

Climate change adaptation also connects to a general debate revolving around the Norwegian term *samfunnssikkerhet* (societal safety and security). The debate focuses on safeguarding society from major threats such as natural disasters, pandemics, cyberattacks, or terrorism, with the overarching goal of ensuring public safety and maintaining essential societal functions. The concept is grounded in a policy that revolves around four key principles: responsibility, proximity, similarity, and cooperation. These principles guide the efforts of various stakeholders, including the Ministry of Justice and Public Security, the Norwegian Directorate for Civil Protection, municipalities, police, and private sector actors.

According to Morsut (2020), the Norwegian approach to *samfunnssikkerhet* reflects a balance between national adaptations and shared Nordic principles, providing a framework for navigating an increasingly complex and dynamic security landscape. By prioritising equality, the clear delineation of responsibilities, and local-level management, the concept ensures that crises are addressed equitably and efficiently. Additionally, its holistic emphasis on collaboration fosters strong cooperation among all stakeholders, ideally enhancing Norway's capacity to respond to and recover from diverse security challenges. Morsut (2020) highlights the evolution of Nordic societal security from Cold War-era civil defence to addressing contemporary challenges such as terrorism, cyber threats, and climate change. The development of *samfunnssikkerhet* in Norway closely aligns with this trajectory, with the 2011 terrorist attacks in Oslo and Utøya serving as a defining moment.

Burgess (2024), in contrast, examines societal security and safety in Norway as an interplay between material processes and deeper ethical, cultural, and spiritual dimensions. He emphasises that security extends beyond safeguarding infrastructure or implementing technical measures. Rather, it encompasses a broader understanding of how societal values, community cohesion, and collective identity shape both the perception of threats and the strategies employed to address them. On a material level, societal safety and security encompass physical infrastructure, logistical measures, and bureaucratic systems, framing security as a technical issue managed through emergency responses, critical infrastructure protection, and coordinated actions. However, Burgess also highlights the ethical dimensions intertwined with societal safety and security. According to Burgess, cultural identity emerges as central to security, with a cognitive dimension addressing society's intrinsic moral and existential foundations. Collective discourses and symbolic acts reaffirm shared values and community resilience. Furthermore, the dual role of society as both protector and protected underscores its vulnerability to threats while serving as a source of cohesion, solidarity, and security. This duality reflects the interdependence of structural mechanisms and intangible societal qualities, as threats often stem from tensions within liberal societies' own value systems.

The Norwegian approach to societal safety and security prioritises the protection of critical societal functions and democratic values, aligning closely with Burgess's view of security as a construct shaped by social and political dynamics rather than objective realities. For instance, Norway's response to crises demonstrates how societal resilience is cultivated through public trust and cultural cohesion rather than relying solely on technical or militarised measures. Such dynamics were evident during the 2005 Hatlestad landslide and the 2023 storm Hans, where responses emphasised localised coordination, the rapid mobilisation of civil protection resources, and clear communication from authorities, reinforcing trust in governance while avoiding overdramatisation or securitised rhetoric. These events showcased the importance of institutional readiness and community-based responses in managing climate-related and geophysical threats, where the perception of safety was shaped as much by political handling and cultural framing as by physical risk.

Similarly, Burgess's focus on the 'analytics of government' highlights the role of institutional tools, administrative mechanisms, and practices in security governance, paralleling Norway's emphasis on risk governance, preparedness, and infrastructure redundancy as central pillars of societal safety and security. Both approaches recognise the ethical implications of securitisation, emphasising the importance of avoiding over-securitisation, which can threaten societal cohesion and democratic values. Together, these perspectives advocate for a holistic approach to safety and security, balancing material preparedness with the preservation of cultural, ethical, and societal integrity to ensure legitimacy and effectiveness.

Societal safety and security reveal how legitimacy is not only about technical competence or administrative design, but also about values, perceptions, and social meaning. Indeed, the Norwegian model of societal safety and security, as described by Morsut (2020) and Burgess (2024), draws on all three of Scharpf's dimensions (1999): local responsiveness and trust (input), coordinated and transparent governance (throughput), and effective crisis management (output). At the same time, it reflects Suchman's types of legitimacy (1995): it is pragmatic in solving real threats, moral in its commitment to equality and democratic values, and increasingly cognitive, as societal security becomes an unquestioned imperative in the face of emerging risks like climate change and cyber threats. In this way, legitimacy becomes both a driver and a product of how societal safety is governed, shaping the structural design of frameworks and reinforcing the normative idea of what the state is and what it should be.

An important consideration regarding the legitimacy issue rests in societal safety and security. Keeping the population, the economy, or national infrastructure safe resonates with ideas about what the state is: safeguarding a nation's security is an essential task for any state (Leffler, 1990). Such argumentation provides a normative platform for understanding what climate change adaptation is about in the context of managing climate risks and observed natural hazards. Hence, the societal safety and security framing of climate change adaptation not only reflects particular instrumental needs but also the broader definition of the state itself.

5.6 Conclusion

Climate change adaptation in the Norwegian context involves three semi-distinct areas: a statutory planning regime that places responsibilities at the local level; a techno-administrative regime that emphasises schematic approaches to risk and a technical orientation in the application of knowledge; and a societal safety and security framing that delineates the salience of threats and responses. These three areas reflect discourses where different actors engage in forwarding distinct types of arguments, but where there is also an inevitable overlap between governance arrangements, practices, and tools. As Norwegian actors strive to establish governance capacity, these three discourses reflect an approach to legitimising their actions that is marked by complexity. No singular legitimation strategy is evident; instead, combinations of legitimation efforts cut across all categories suggested by the analytical framework (Table 5.1).

Some patterns nevertheless emerge. On the one hand, it seems the legitimation of climate change adaptation approaches becomes more complex when the arena for the discourse is associated with a higher level of governance. Whereas the relatively localised techno-administrative discourse seems to lend a focus towards pragmatic, throughput-oriented concerns, the planning discourse—connecting national ambitions to local planning—seems to be emphasising legitimacy concerns that are both input- and throughput-directed and pragmatic and moral in orientation. The wider societal security discourse, however, straddles all three legitimation directions (input, throughput, output) and all three types of content (pragmatic, moral, cognitive).

On the other hand, the relative weight of the direction and content of legitimation rationales differs. Although the societal safety and security discourse in many respects includes more than the other two areas, it is also a discourse at a more generalised level that is more loosely coupled to practices. Hence, the role of cognitive framings of the narrative can play out more as a political argument than is the case for the statutory, judicial framing of planning and the pragmatically oriented technological-administrative discourse. Conversely, the problem-solving rationales of technological-administrative arrangements and practices suggest recipes and templates, engineering, and estimation that differ markedly in terms of desired output from those of societal security or local democratic societal planning. The planning discourse operates across local and national domains, combining pragmatic concerns with core societal values. This shows how legitimation discourses may be characterized by different levels of generality and abstraction.

Importantly, legitimation discourses are not only about what actors *say*; they are also about what they *do*. Evidently, the three discourses of Norwegian climate change adaptation reflect an organised approach marked by specific divisions of functions and responsibilities. A topic for future inquiries rests with the intersections between adaptation issues and other societal concerns that also inhabit the planning domain, the techno-administrative approach, and the debate on societal safety and security. Arguably, one of the main criticisms of climate change adaptation policies

Table 5.1 Legitimation strategies in Norwegian climate change adaptation discourses

	Statutory planning discourse	*Techno-administrative discourse*	*Societal safety discourse*
Legitimation direction	Input, throughput, output	Throughput	Input, throughput, output
Legitimation content	Moral	Pragmatic, moral	Pragmatic, cognitive, moral

in Norway has been the observation that it is embedded with so many other issues: planning is more than adaptation; it is also a matter of local democracy and developing local communities. Technical solutions to adaptation problems are adjustments necessary for providing infrastructure. Societal safety and security connects to discourses about the wider threats towards modern society, whether local or global.

Some stakeholders have argued for a separate ministerial post for climate adaptation that supposedly can cut across these complexities by leveraging top-down authority and setting the political agenda. Such an approach would perhaps be a move towards a stronger focus on threats and would have to rest on a different set of legitimation efforts than the ones observed as is. An open question, regardless of legitimation efforts, is whether the small-scale wickedness of climate change adaptation (Neby, 2019) could be resolved by such an approach. Climate change adaptation, it seems, is about foundational ideas of what is important; it is about the political-administrative procedures and measures implemented; it is about problem-solving and preparedness; and it is everywhere.

Our discussion about the discourses and legitimation practices in Norwegian climate change adaptation gives indications about governance capacity, legitimacy, and possible legitimacy challenges. Both governance capacity and governance legitimacy are relevant indicators of how a country, in general, deals with risks and crises. The climate change adaptation policy field in Norway has been framed as crossing policies and sectoral boundaries, not because of a deliberate policy design, but because complexity reflects the precise nature of the climate change adaptation challenge.

References

Booth, L., Fleming, K., Abad, J., Schueller, L. A., Leone, M., Scolobig, A., & Baills, A. (2020). Simulating synergies between climate change adaptation and disaster risk reduction stakeholders to improve management of transboundary disasters in Europe. *International Journal of Disaster Risk Reduction, 49*, 101668.

Burgess, J. P. (2024). *Security after the unthinkable: Terror and disenchantment in Norway*. Manchester University Press.

Christensen, T., & Lægreid, P. (2020). Balancing governance capacity and legitimacy: How the Norwegian government handled the COVID-19 crisis as a high performer. *Public Administration Review, 80*(5), 774–779.

Christensen, T., Lægreid, P., & Rykkja, L. H. (2016). Organizing for crisis management: Building governance capacity and legitimacy. *Public Administration Review, 76*(6), 887–897.

Christensen, T., Lægreid, P., & Rykkja, L. H. (2019). Organizing for societal security and crisis management: Governance capacity and legitimacy. In P. Lægreid & L. H. Rykkja (Eds.), *Societal security and crisis management: Governance capacity and legitimacy* (pp. 1–23). Palgrave Macmillan.

Dannevig, H., Hovelsrud, G. K., & Husabø, I. A. (2013). Driving the agenda for climate change adaptation in Norwegian municipalities. *Environment and Planning. C, Government & Policy, 31*(3), 490–505.

Dellmuth, L., & Gustafsson, M. T. (2023). Legitimacy in the trans-scalar governance of climate adaptation. *Npj Climate Action, 2*(1), 2.

Diez, T., Von Lucke, F., & Wellmann, Z. (2016). *The securitisation of climate change: Actors, processes and consequences.* Routledge.

DSB. (2022). *Veileder til helhetlig risiko- og sårbarhetsanalyse i kommunen En metodeveileder for helhetlig ROS i kommunal beredskapsplikt.* Direktoratet for samfunnssikkerhet og beredskap (DSB).

Dunn, W. N. (1990). Justifying policy arguments: Criteria for practical discourse. *Evaluation and Program Planning, 13*(3), 321–329.

Eriksen, S. H., Nightingale, A. J., & Eakin, H. (2015). Reframing adaptation: The political nature of climate change adaptation. *Global Environmental Change, 35*, 523–533.

Few, R., Brown, K., & Tompkins, E. L. (2007). Public participation and climate change adaptation: Avoiding the illusion of inclusion. *Climate Policy, 7*(1), 46–59.

Hanssen-Bauer, I., Førland, E. J., Haddeland, I., Hisdal, H., Lawrence, D., Mayer, S., Nesje, A., Nilsen, J. E. Ø., Sandven, S., Sandø, A. B., Sorteberg, A., & Ådlandsvik, B. (2017). *Climate in Norway 2100 – A knowledge base for climate adaptation. NCCs report 1/17.* Norwegian Centre for Climate Services.

Karlson, C. W., Morsut, C., & Engen, O. A. H. (2023). Politics of climate risk management in local government: A case study of the municipality of Stavanger. *Frontiers in Climate, 5*, 1136673.

Klein, J., Mäntysalo, R., & Juhola, S. (2016). Legitimacy of urban climate change adaptation: A case in Helsinki. *Regional Environmental Change, 16*(3), 815–826.

Kvamsås, H. (2022). *The potential for transformative adaptation: Collaborative spaces and collective value development in local climate adaptation.* PhD dissertation, University of Bergen.

Leffler, M. P. (1990). National security. *The Journal of American History, 77*(1), 143–152.

Lempert, R., Nakicenovic, N., Sarewitz, D., & Schlesinger, M. (2004). Characterizing climate-change uncertainties for decision-makers. *Climatic Change, 65*, 1–9. https://doi.org/10.1023/B:CLIM.0000037561.75281.b3

Lie, L. B., Lysgaard, V., & Sydnes, A. K. (2024). Anticipating climate risk in Norwegian municipalities. *Climate Risk Management, 46*, 100658.

Lodge, M., & Wegrich, K. (Eds.). (2014). *The problem-solving capacity of the modern state: Governance challenges and administrative capacities.* Oxford University Press.

Lund-Tønnesen, J. (2025). Privacy regimes, crisis strategies, and governments' legitimizing of digital surveillance technology: Comparing Germany, Norway, and the United Kingdom. *International Journal of Public Administration, 48*(5–6), 381–394.

Mees, H. L., Driessen, P. P., & Runhaar, H. A. (2012). Exploring the scope of public and private responsibilities for climate adaptation. *Journal of Environmental Policy & Planning, 14*(3), 305–330.

Meld. St. 26 (2022–2023). (2023). *Klima i endring – sammen for et robust samfunn.* Det kongelige klima- og miljødepartement.

Meld. St. 33 (2012–2013). (2013). *Klimatilpasning i Norge.* Det kongelige miljøverndepartement.

Morsut, C. (2020). The emergence and development of *samfunnssikkerhet* in Norway. In S. Larsson & M. Rhinard (Eds.), *A Nordic model for societal security? Convergence and divergence* (pp. 68–90). Routledge.

Morsut, C., Engen, O. A., Neby, S., & Angell, E. (2024). Translations of climate change consequences at the local level: Climate change adaptation in Bergen and Stavanger municipalities in Norway. *Risk, Hazards & Crisis in Public Policy, 15*(4), 468–490.

Neby, S. (2019). Climate adaptation and preparedness in Norway: Third order effects, small-scale wickedness and governance capacity. *International Public Management Review, 19*(2), 26–46.

Neby, S., Engen, O. A., Morsut, C., & Angell, E. (2023a). Klimakrisen, klimarisiko og innrammingen av norsk klimapolitikk. *Stat & Styring, 33*(2), 16–21.

Neby, S., Angell, E., Engen, O. A., & Morsut, C. (2023b). Klimatilpasning i Norge: Mellom risiko, beredskap og normalsituasjon. *Norsk statsvitenskapelig tidsskrift, 39*(4), 159–176.

NOU 2018:18. (2018). *Klimarisiko og norsk økonomi.* Official Norwegian Report.

Orderud, G. I., & Naustdalslid, J. (2019). Climate change adaptation in Norway: Learning–knowledge processes and the demand for transformative adaptation. *International Journal of Sustainable Development and World Ecology, 27*(1), 15–27.

Remling, E. (2018). Depoliticizing adaptation: A critical analysis of EU climate adaptation policy. *Environmental Politics, 27*(3), 477–497.

Rhinard, M., Morsut, C., Angell, E., Neby, S., Englund, M., Barquet, K., Mees, H., Surian, J., Vashishtha, S., Segnestam, L., & Hegland Engen, O. A. (2024). Understanding variation in national climate change adaptation: Securitization in focus. *Environment and Planning C: Politics and Spaces, 42*(4), 676–696. https://doi.org/10.1177/23996544231212730

Rød, J. K., Selseng, T., & Aall, C. (2025). *Kommunerangeringen 2024. Klimarisiko, Norsk Klimamonitor*. Accessed June 25, 2025, from https://klimamonitor.no/klimarisiko/kommunerangeringa

Scharpf, F. (1999). *Governing in Europe: Effective and democratic?* Oxford University Press.

Schmidt, V., & Wood, M. (2019). Conceptualizing throughput legitimacy: Procedural mechanisms of accountability, transparency, inclusiveness and openness in EU governance. *Public Administration, 97*(4), 727–740.

Shanahan, E. A., Jones, M. D., McBeth, M. K., & Lane, R. R. (2013). An angel on the wind: How heroic policy narratives shape policy realities. *Policy Studies Journal, 41*(3), 453–483.

Suchman, M. C. (1995). Managing legitimacy: Strategic and institutional approaches. *Academy of Management Review, 20*(3), 571–610.

Sygna, L., O'Brien, K., & Wolf, J. (2013). *A changing environment for human security*. Earthscan.

van Buuren, A., Driessen, P., Teisman, G., & van Rijswick, M. (2014). Toward legitimate governance strategies for climate adaptation in the Netherlands: Combining insights from a legal, planning, and network perspective. *Regional Environmental Change, 14*, 1021–1033.

Wejs, A., Harvold, K., Larsen, S. V., & Saglie, I.-L. (2014). Legitimacy building in weak institutional settings: Climate change adaptation at the local level in Denmark and Norway. *Environmental Politics, 23*(3), 490–508.

Westskog, H., Hovelsrud, G. K., & Sundqvist, G. (2017). How to make local context matter in national advice: Towards adaptive comanagement in Norwegian climate adaptation. *Weather, Climate, and Society, 9*(2), 267–283.

CHAPTER 6

On Flood Risk and the Relationship Between Climate Change Adaptation, Prevention, and Preparedness

Claudia Morsut, Ole Andreas Engen, and Bjørn Ivar Kruke

Abstract Floods have become a major climate risk in many countries causing severe material damage to homes, roads, bridges, and other critical infrastructure. The purpose of this chapter is to discuss the relationship between climate change adaptation, prevention and preparedness in the context of flood risk management. Climate change adaptation concerns societal development and includes both preventive measures to reduce the likelihood of unwanted events and preparedness measures to lessen the

This chapter was previously published as 'Om flomrisiko og sammenhengen mellom forebygging og beredskap innenfor klimatilpasning', in the December 2024 Norwegian anthology *Flom, skred og juss*, edited by Steinar Taubøll. We thank the editor for allowing us to use the chapter, which has been translated with the support of Co-Pilot and subject to language editing. It has been rearranged to better adhere to the scope of this book.

C. Morsut (✉) • O. A. Engen • B. I. Kruke
University of Stavanger, Stavanger, Norway
e-mail: claudia.morsut@uis.no; ole.a.engen@uis.no; bjorn.i.kruke@uis.no

C. Morsut (ed.), *Adapting to Climate Change*,
https://doi.org/10.1007/978-3-032-07136-1_6

consequences of those events that are not preventable. However, uncertainty in climate forecasts—especially locally, where municipalities have a central role in climate change adaptation—makes it difficult to carry out risk assessments and analyses that can form the basis for prevention and preparedness and, consequently, for adaptation measures. In addition, there exist challenges linked to municipalities' capacity to take a risk-based approach to prevention and preparedness. Future extreme weather events and the need for climate change adaptation will place greater demands on risk and vulnerability analyses, legislation, and societal planning, as well as on municipalities' capacity to handle events related to a changing climate.

Keywords Climate change adaptation • Flood risk • Preparedness • Prevention • Residual risk • Risk and vulnerability analysis • Uncertainty

6.1 Introduction

One of the most striking climate risks is flood risk, which has become a frequent climatic phenomenon across Europe (Alfieri et al., 2016) and globally (Alfieri et al., 2015). Floods have devastating effects: they endanger lives and ecosystems, damage critical infrastructure, reduce biodiversity, and often result in significant economic losses. Norway is a country that has become particularly vulnerable to flood risks (Aaheim, 2009). Indeed, the climate profile of Norway, provided by the Norwegian Climate Services Centre (Norsk klimaservicesenter, 2025), indicates that the annual precipitation will increase, and, especially in summer, the country will experience more frequent and intense heavy rainfall events. Due to the rising temperature, rapid snowmelt will become more common, increasing flood risk, while coastal areas, especially in southern and western Norway, will be more exposed to storm surges and coastal flooding (Hanssen-Bauer et al., 2016).

Destructive floods are not new to Norway. The country has experienced several major floods in recent decades, notably in 1967, 1987, and 1995 (Aaheim, 2009). What is relatively new is the attribution of the increased flood risk to climate change. One of the most recent flood events happened in August 2023, when an extreme weather event called Hans brought exceptionally heavy rainfall to parts of southern Norway. According to the Norwegian Meteorological Institute (MET, 2023), the precipitation levels were the highest recorded in the past 25 years. However, challenges associated with Hans were not solely caused by the extreme weather, but also by other challenges concerning climate risk prevention and preparedness, legitimacy, responsibilities, and the use of resources, which all affected climate change adaptation.

This chapter aims to explore the relationship between climate change adaptation, prevention, and preparedness in the context of flood risk management in Norway. Risk management encompasses both prevention and preparedness, as it provides the conceptual and procedural framework through which risks are identified, assessed, and addressed. Prevention and preparedness are distinct but complementary processes: prevention aims to reduce the likelihood of harmful events, while preparedness focuses on enhancing the capacity to respond effectively if such events occur. As integral components of the risk management cycle—which includes risk identification, analysis, evaluation, treatment, monitoring, and communication—prevention and preparedness are prioritised, balanced, and integrated in relation to identified risks, acceptable risk levels, and available resources. Risk management thus enables informed decision making under conditions of uncertainty and ensures coherence between prevention and preparedness by aligning them with organisational or societal risk tolerance and overarching societal objectives. We argue that, while climate change adaptation primarily consists of preventive actions, the presence of residual risk—risk that remains after preventive measures have been implemented (UNDRR, 2017a)—necessitates the inclusion of preparedness measures to address not only the uncertainty associated with future extreme weather events, but also the residual risk that preventive adaptation measures cannot fully deter. The relationship between prevention and preparedness is, thus, characterised by both uncertainty and residual risk, which complicate risk assessments and analyses needed to inform effective measures in adaptation.

Adaptation is executed primarily at the municipal level, as Chap. 5 reveals. Local actors are crucial since they possess knowledge and expertise that can inform risk analyses and decision making. Managing climate risks requires detailed and localised risk descriptions to determine the degree of complexity, uncertainty, and ambiguity, and to develop appropriate instruments capable of addressing these risks. The 2023 Total Preparedness Commission (NOU, 2023:17, 2023) acknowledges the role of Norwegian municipalities in climate change adaptation but also highlights both preparedness limitations and challenges related to their capacity and ability to manage crises. The Commission emphasises the state's role as a guide and coordinator and the importance of close collaboration between national agencies (directorates, ministries, county governors) and local experts to develop and implement adaptation measures to reduce risks. However, the Commission is less explicit about the distribution of responsibilities and resources between the state and municipalities and the uncertainties associated with complex coordination structures.

Flood risk is a systemic and multi-dimensional climate risk and is not only shaped by climate change-induced events, like precipitation and snowmelt, but is also influenced by social, institutional, and political factors that affect exposure and vulnerability. In Norway, climate change is intensifying flood risk, but governance challenges, such as inadequate societal planning and mismatches between municipal responsibilities and resources, exacerbate the problem. Drawing on insights from Chaps. 2, 3, and 5, this chapter highlights how flood risk is increasingly managed through technocratic practices that may obscure deeper questions of power, legitimacy, and justice. Flood risk governance in Norway demands more than technical solutions—it requires adaptive, inclusive, and politically aware approaches to cope with uncertainty and ensure effective adaptation.

6.2 Climate Change Adaptation, Prevention, and Preparedness: An Inextricable Relationship

As pointed out in the introduction of this book, climate change adaptation includes a wide array of measures, practices, and strategies to adjust to climate change by reducing climate risks (IPCC, 2023, p. 7). The Norwegian National Planning Guidelines for Climate and Energy Planning and Climate Change Adaptation (Regulation, 2018) emphasise that climate change adaptation efforts must help society become more resilient to climate change by ensuring that municipalities and counties avoid or reduce risk, vulnerability, and current and future climate impacts. The guidelines also stress that climate change adaptation is a cross-sectoral task requiring coordination and cooperation across sectors and between municipal, county, and national authorities. National agencies are expected to collect, organise, and disseminate climate knowledge for use in planning.

Two additional public documents outline the relevance of adaptation in reducing climate risks in general and flood risks in particular. The first one is *White Paper No. 26 (2022–2023), Climate in Change – Together for a Climate-Resilient Society* (Meld. St. 26 (2022–2023), 2023), which was published just months before Hans. This White Paper offers a general overview of the Norwegian climate change policy. Specific measures are proposed to improve flood risk management, such as better use of nature-based solutions, adjustments to the natural disaster insurance scheme, stricter building requirements in the Planning and Building Act to increase security from hazards induced by climate change, and risk prevention. The document states that flood protection should be used wherever appropriate and calls for ways to better integrate preventive measures in dealing with climate risks. The White Paper also announced a new White Paper on floods and landslides, as the previous one dated back to 2012 (Meld. St. 15 (2011–2012), 2012). In that earlier document, it was emphasised that certain responsibilities mandated to municipalities were unclear.

The new White Paper, *White Paper No. 27 (2023–2024), A Safer Future – Preparedness for Floods and Landslides* (Meld. St. 27 (2023–2024), 2024) was published in May 2024 and is dedicated to flood and landslide risks. It addresses all phases of flood and landslide risk management, from prevention and emergency response to post-event recovery. It emphasises the need to strengthen preventive efforts, including protective measures, mapping, spatial planning, monitoring, and early warning systems to enhance resilience.

All three documents consider adaptation as involving emergency preparedness for specific events such as floods or landslides and emphasise land-use planning, nature-based solutions, or new technologies. In essence, climate change adaptation aims to boost resilience through solutions that allow Norwegian society to resist, absorb, accommodate, adapt to, transform, and recover from the effects of a hazard in a timely and efficient manner (UNDRR, 2017b). These solutions integrate the prevention of possible unwanted events damaging society, consisting of activities and measures to avoid existing and new climate risks (UNDRR, 2017c), and preparedness to deal with events that are not preventable. Prevention encompasses reducing both the vulnerability of society and infrastructure and exposure to climate risks. In the specific case of flood risks, preventive initiatives may include dams to stop flash floods following extreme rainfall, embankments as barriers along rivers to avoid flooding, and societal planning and regulation on land use to avoid constructing infrastructure and houses in vulnerable areas.

Although societies invest resources in prevention, this is only part of the solution, as prevention is often related to preparedness, which aims to effectively anticipate, respond to, and recover from the impacts of likely, imminent, or ongoing disaster events (UNDRR, 2017d). Like prevention, preparedness requires sound risk and vulnerability analyses (RVAs) on climate risks. Preparedness, one of the main activities in the pre-crisis phase (Kruke, 2012), includes activities such as preparedness analysis for assessing preparedness according to risks assessed in the RVAs, contingency planning, securing relevant and adequate equipment, facilitating systems and arrangements for information sharing, coordination, cooperation, crisis communication, early warning procedures, evacuation plans, and relevant training and exercises. All these preparedness activities need to be formalised in legislation, directives, and instructions.

We illustrate this interplay between adaptation, prevention and preparedness by using a bowtie figure (see De Ruijter & Guldenmund, 2016) that considers flood risk management.

Figure 6.1 illustrates the relationship between potential causes of flood risk and the measures that can be implemented to avoid its main consequence, a flood. The purpose of these measures is to reduce both the likelihood of the flood occurring (prevention) and the severity of its impacts (preparedness). The undesirable event—the flood—is placed at the centre of the figure. Potential causes leading to the flood are positioned on the left side of the figure, while possible consequences of the flood are on the right side. Measures that can help prevent or limit the likelihood of the flood and measures that can reduce its consequences are represented as vertical columns, respectively, to the left and right of the centre of the figure.

Prevention and preparedness measures represent barriers, which can be technical and physical (e.g. levees, drainage systems) or organisational and

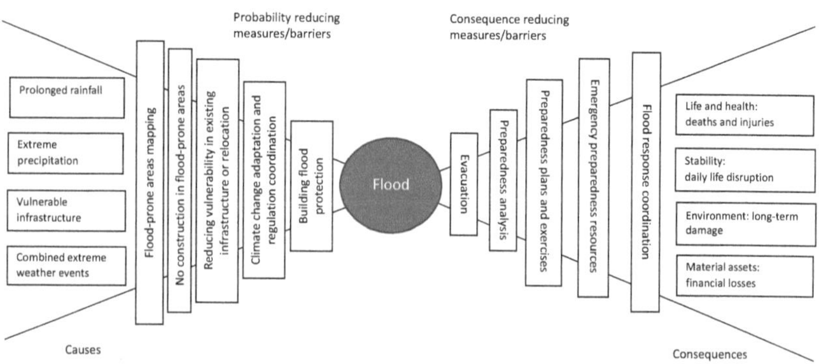

Fig. 6.1 Illustration of interplay between adaptation, prevention, and preparedness in flood risk management (by authors)

institutional (e.g. legislation, regulations, technical standards, training, and exercises). The consequences of a flood can lead to cascading effects in other areas, resulting in significant societal impacts. For example, a breach in flood defences could damage power lines and roads, resulting in power outages and the isolation of affected communities. The challenge lies in reducing flood risk through effective preventive measures, such as embankments along rivers and regulations on how much water energy companies can release during a flood.

Adaptation aims at reducing flood risk through preventive actions. However, the embedded uncertainty necessitates the inclusion of preparedness measures to address the uncertainty associated with future extreme weather events, which preventive adaptation measures cannot entirely deter. Residual risk remains after all feasible preventive measures have been implemented, and it is heavily influenced by the uncertainty inherent in predicting future weather events. Despite advances in meteorological modelling, uncertainty in forecasting extreme weather means that some residual risk will always remain. The greater the uncertainty in climate projections, the more difficult it becomes to reduce residual risk to acceptable levels. Residual risk is thus a potent reminder that regardless of the preventive adaptation measures, unexpected impacts require preparedness measures, such as contingency plans. Regardless of how much we invest in preventive measures to reduce flood risks, there will always be a residual risk, whether due to financial constraints, the need to balance risk reduction with other considerations, or uncertainty in risk assessments. In this context, institutions, politics, culture, and values become crucial for those conducting risk assessments and making decisions to evaluate what constitutes an acceptable level of risk.

Put simply, the relationship between prevention and preparedness is characterised by significant uncertainty, which complicates the risk assessments and analyses needed to inform effective adaptation measures. When viewed through the lens of the risk definition (see Chap. 2), flood risk refers to the uncertainty associated with flood events that affect societal vulnerabilities, including life, health, and infrastructure. This uncertainty also concerns whether existing preparedness measures are sufficient to manage the event and whether there is an adequate set of consequence-reducing measures in place.

6.3 Flood Risk in Norway: Definition, Management, and Governance

The projections provided by the Norwegian Climate Services Centre are quite accurate and clearly indicate that flood risk is a reality that must be addressed with no delay. However, flood risk is not purely climate-driven, as we note in the introduction of this chapter: development in vulnerable areas, ageing infrastructure, demographic trends, and historically rooted land-use decisions and regulations also play a major role. As a multi-dimensional and systemic climate risk, flood risk is not merely a consequence of climate change but a product of the layered interaction between physical dynamics (like precipitation, snowmelt, and sea-level rise) and social, institutional, and political systems that determine exposure and vulnerability (see Chap. 3).

We aim here to define flood risk, which means we must refer to relevant classifications for evaluating risks. Ortwin Renn (2008) proposes a classification that links the potential for harm with the likelihood of occurrence. He distinguishes between linear, complex, uncertain, and ambiguous risks, each of which requires a different analytical approach. Linear risks refer to relatively well-known events and situations with abundant data that can be analysed using widely accepted risk assessment methods. Complex risks involve phenomena where it is difficult to determine the relationships between multiple causes and observed effects. Uncertain risks signal phenomena where it is challenging to predict events and their consequences, often due to a genuine lack of knowledge—what we might call ignorance. Examples include major natural disasters (e.g. tsunamis), new viruses, and bacteria. The degree of uncertainty can vary. Some risks are known unknowns, while others are unknown unknowns—often referred to as black swans (Taleb, 2010; see also Chap. 3). Risks are often multifaceted, making it difficult to determine who should be responsible and at what level. Typically, multiple stakeholders are involved in risk management processes, leading to disagreements, power struggles, and conflicts over priorities, organisation, and decision-making.

Drawing on Ortwin Renn's risk typology (2008), flood risk can be characterised as complex, due to the interplay of hydrological, infrastructural, environmental, and societal variables; uncertain, since, while climate projections and models forecast more frequent and intense precipitation, local manifestations—timing, intensity, cascading effects—remain unpredictable; and ambiguous, since actors such as municipalities, national agencies, landowners, and insurers interpret flood risks differently, leading to divergent priorities and governance challenges. This classification makes flood risk a governance issue as much as a management one.

In Norway, national legislation provides a formal framework through instruments like the Planning and Building Act (Plan- og bygningsloven, 2008) and the Civil Protection Act (Sivilbeskyttelsesloven, 2010). As shown in Chap. 5, these two key laws endow municipalities with the responsibility for land-use management and emergency preparedness in Norway, both with direct and indirect impacts on flood risks. The Planning and Building Act applies to all land areas in Norway, including water resources and watercourses. Under this act, municipalities play a central role as planning authorities and are expected to integrate adaptation measures into planning. They must facilitate participation from relevant agencies and stakeholders. Counties are encouraged to promote collaboration and learning through regional planning forums. Sectoral authorities with overlapping responsibilities must assess the need for coordination in planning processes. As much as public actors, private actors must comply with requirements concerning the use and protection of land. The Planning and Building Act addresses society's relationship with nature and the environment in several places, including in regulations such as the national planning guidelines introduced in 2018. It outlines how planning should be conducted, the responsibilities of various actors, how participation should be ensured, and the principles that apply. With its broad scope, the act provides the framework for politically guided societal development and sets both substantive and procedural guidelines for municipal priorities.

The Civil Protection Act governs how the emergency preparedness system is organised in Norway and how to protect 'life, the environment, infrastructure, and other values against war, natural disasters, and other undesirable events' (§1). Municipalities are legally obligated to maintain emergency preparedness under this law, including conducting comprehensive RVAs to identify potential hazards and damages (§14). RVAs have become particularly important for planning, prevention, and preparedness at the municipal level. In these analyses, several types of risks are assessed, including those derived from climate change. Climate risks are thus assessed within a framework with more general ambitions than assessing climate risks alone. RVAs often inform climate change adaptation (Karlson et al., 2023; Neby et al., 2023a), which becomes part of broader political priorities concerning societal development.

In Norway, there is no specific climate risk management agency; instead, relevant work is generally integrated into existing risk management frameworks (see NOU, 2018:17, 2018, p. 123), such as the RVAs. In addition, municipalities are responsible for ensuring safe construction, verifying flood safety, and complying with technical standards, which requires significant knowledge, competence, and often dedicated climate budgets. For instance, municipalities are bound to follow technical building regulations (TEK 17, 2025) that set the minimum standards that a structure must meet to be legally constructed in Norway. Chapter 7 of these regulations addresses safety against natural hazards, including floods, and defines three safety classes for buildings located in flood-prone areas. Buildings critical to national or regional emergency preparedness and crisis management, such as hospitals and national emergency institutions, must not be in flood-prone areas if flooding would compromise their functionality. The aim of these restrictions is to ensure that such facilities remain operational during major incidents. In addition, the regulations provide measures to follow, such as flood-proofing the structure or designing and constructing the building to withstand flood-related stresses.

This legislation clearly foresees that municipalities carry out both prevention and preparedness to address a wide range of risks, including flood risks. However, responsibility is often not matched with resources, producing a fundamental imbalance in Norway's multi-level governance system. Municipalities face challenges related to funding, capacity, and coordination (Morsut et al., 2024; Neby et al., 2023b; Neby, 2019), but they lie at the bottom of a governance web of numerous national departments. The Ministry of Energy oversees flood and landslide management, among its several tasks. The Norwegian Water Resources and Energy Directorate (under the Ministry of Energy) is the national expert authority on water and energy resources and provides flood zone maps for municipal planning. The Ministry of Justice and Public Security is responsible for civil protection and emergency preparedness, while its main agency, the Directorate for Civil Protection, monitors national risks and vulnerabilities and develops standards for emergency planning. The Ministry of Climate and Environment and its Environment Agency coordinate climate adaptation and water regulations. The Ministry of Local Government and Regional Development oversees planning legislation and municipal finances, while its Directorate for Building Quality ensures compliance with building safety standards (e.g. TEK17). County governors monitor national goals and their implementation at the municipal level. Four principles—responsibility, proximity, similarity, and cooperation—drive the complex work in prevention and preparedness.

A report by the Office of the General Auditor of Norway highlights the challenges municipalities face in meeting formal requirements, especially as many municipal plans are outdated and based on pre-2012 flood maps that do not account for climate change. The report concludes that coordination between national and local authorities is also weak, and the knowledge base for assessing climate change adaptation is insufficient (Riksrevisjonen, 2025).

6.4 Challenges in Climate Change Adaptation, Prevention, and Preparedness

In this chapter, we explored the relationship between climate change adaptation, prevention, and preparedness using flood risk as a type of risk where this relationship is relevant. The bowtie model served as an illustration to pinpoint how the three phenomena are intertwined. The legislation presented above includes prevention as well as preparedness requirements that municipalities need to fulfil to cope with risks in general and with climate risks in particular, including flood risks. These frameworks governing prevention and preparedness in Norway are complex and multifaceted, offering both opportunities and limitations for managing flood risk through adaptive measures. Risk and vulnerability analyses form the foundation for both preventive and preparedness efforts aimed at managing uncertainty. However, prevention and preparedness are embedded in laws and regulations that place significant demands on municipalities, not only before, during, and after natural events, but also in terms of acquiring competences that are often difficult to meet due to limited financial and organisational resources.

This leads to two challenges for adaptation, one related to risk management, the other to governance.

First, the national frameworks assume that climate change adaptation manages climate change mainly in terms of risk prevention and that national adaptation requirements can be translated into local emergency plans. White Paper 27 (2023–2024) emphasises the importance of strengthening preventive efforts related to flooding and calls for the development of a more comprehensive risk picture across different types of floods. Yet, the terminology used in the White Paper, such as probability and consequence, reflects outdated risk concepts (see Chap. 2). Given the uncertainty associated with climate change and climate risk (as also highlighted by the IPCC; see Chap. 4), it is surprising that the White Paper does not incorporate more advanced methodological references to risk, especially considering the new requirements for the RVAs, as indicated by the new guidelines introduced by the Directorate for Civil Protection and Emergency Preparedness in 2022 (DSB, 2022).

The term risk in legal texts and regulations is often applied to natural hazards (e.g. landslides, floods, surface water, invasive species), which may involve economic, societal, health, or infrastructure risks. These documents tend to rely on a static definition of flood risk, which does not adequately account for climate projections. In other words, the uncertainty posed by future climate change is not sufficiently integrated into the knowledge base for decision-making. To address this, RVAs should be based on a dynamic risk picture that includes qualitative assessments alongside quantitative data. RVAs can be improved, including not only solid data but also critical reflections on the knowledge base that those data represent. Uncertainty assessments must be a mandatory part of the analysis, acknowledging that the uncertainty is inherently tied to governance challenges, legitimacy, responsibility distribution, and coordination, whether in prevention or preparedness.

Here, we can envisage a paradox: while legislation often describes procedures and responsibilities in general terms, climate change adaptation requires place-specific and cross-sectoral trade-offs that municipalities cannot always control. For example, the Planning and Building Act mandates that a 100-metre buffer zone along coastlines and waterways must consider environmental and public interests. It also encourages municipalities to collaborate in regional planning forums. However, how many municipalities in Norway follow these mandates?

There is significant variation between and within municipalities in terms of climate risk and uncertainty. Achieving the right balance between planning, context, and situational awareness is crucial for local adaptation. Since risk is inherently about the future, it is nearly impossible to predict all consequences, especially in a changing climate. As a result, RVAs need to be continuously updated, but this has costs for municipalities, despite their use as a key tool for municipalities to understand and manage risks. To truly benefit from RVAs, municipalities must invest in organisational competence and have the flexibility to act on both prevention and preparedness. Yet, resources and expertise are unevenly distributed across Norwegian municipalities. The result can be incomplete analyses, ineffective adaptation measures, and insufficient preparedness. One challenge is whether municipal RVAs are of sufficient quality to serve as a reliable knowledge base: Do they capture the complexity and provide a holistic perspective on flood risk?

The other significant challenge is related to Norway's multi-level governance system. Laws and regulations outline how actors should cooperate in the face of flood risk and what strategies to use to reduce it. However, flood risk is a type of challenge that municipalities cannot manage alone—they need coordination and support from higher levels, such as the Norwegian Water Resources and Energy Directorate. Although responsibilities are distributed according to the four principles mentioned above, in practice, these principles are challenged by the complexity and uncertainty of flood risk. Since all extreme weather occurs locally, it is natural to assign responsibility to municipalities. However, municipalities are just one of many actors. In Norway, the state has increasingly shifted responsibility for climate risk to the local level. Theoretically, this is correct due to the proximity principle—events should be managed at the lowest possible level, but it undermines the cooperation principle, as constant delegation weakens cooperation. In addition, the proximity principle works only if higher levels of government are constantly engaged with municipalities and understand their needs and challenges, allowing them to provide tailored support. What is needed is professional oversight, coordination, and a structural shift in collaboration that clearly demonstrates the interconnection between flood risk and climate change adaptation.

Major events like the 2023 storm Hans are transboundary, meaning they do not respect administrative boundaries. Therefore, managing flood risk requires close collaboration among a wide range of public, private, and voluntary actors. Post-Hans discussions have focused on insufficient preventive measures along major rivers, inadequate preparedness to manage water volumes, and the need for extensive cooperation in both prevention and emergency response (DSB, 2024). Less attention has been given to the coordination mechanisms necessary for enabling small municipalities to engage in climate change adaptation effectively, meet national requirements, and leverage local knowledge.

Hans revealed the disconnect between governance at the national level and the concrete realities of local RVAs, adaptation measures, and emergency plans. National agencies must be able to recognise local vulnerabilities and provide compensatory support. Support mechanisms from one national agency could help coordinate local resources and connect local actors. A balanced division of labour is needed among municipalities, county governors, and national agencies in terms of knowledge, competence, resources, and planning. Recent floods have also shown the importance of inter-municipal cooperation within the same watershed, both for prevention and preparedness.

To align national expectations with local capabilities, investments in both prevention and preparedness are essential. Moreover, the reliability of the governance system and its mechanisms for managing climate change adaptation must be evaluated. Managing flood risk requires broad cooperation across governance levels and the inclusion of businesses and civil society. In addition, legitimacy emerges as a foundational issue. As discussed in Chap. 5, legal mandates alone do not ensure public trust or acceptance. Legitimacy in flood risk governance involves transparency, inclusivity, and fairness, especially in a context where local authorities are tasked with operationalising national policy under conditions of uncertainty and limited capacity.

6.5 Conclusion

Flood risk exemplifies the uncertainty associated with climate change, as well as residual risk. Uncertainty is not only an inherent quality of flood risks due to climate projections and models, but also due to institutional fragmentation and unclear mandates that shape how prevention and preparedness are organised and implemented. In particular, preparedness should be more than analysis, contingency planning, and equipment or information sharing. It should include adaptive capacities that can respond to unexpected events, like fostering learning systems, scenario-based exercises, and collaborative mechanisms that enable actors to cope with residual risks (see Chap. 3). By its nature, residual risk defies full anticipation and control, making it imperative to prepare for failure in socially just and institutionally robust ways. Acknowledging this according to a Risk Governance perspective allows us to address preparedness not as a *final defence* against residual risk, but as a dynamic and inclusive process which recognises the limits of foresight and prioritises adaptive thinking. Hence, understanding risk management as an overarching framework for prevention and preparedness invites a more nuanced and reflective approach to flood risk governance—one that balances technical assessment with political judgement, and integrates adaptive capacity into the core of climate change adaptation.

Addressing both uncertainty and residual risk requires new competencies across all levels of public administration and increased resources at the municipal level. In Norway, these competencies and resources are not evenly distributed or appropriately aligned to municipal needs, and there is no established mechanism for redistributing them to high-risk areas. Such redistribution must be based on updated risk assessments and future outlooks that can sustain climate change adaptation measures.

The key question is whether current RVAs and the prevailing governance mode concerning prevention and preparedness in Norway are sufficient to grasp the uncertainty that flood risk represents, in addition to the issue of residual risk. Given the high likelihood that flood risk will become an increasing challenge for Norwegian municipalities, their capacity to conduct improved, sound, and independent RVAs will be crucial for implementing adaptation measures. Flood risk management requires providing municipalities with the skills and resources necessary to carry out RVAs and follow up on their results, through a certain degree of dynamicity and flexibility. Local knowledge is essential for managing flood risk, and standardised national requirements can be difficult for individual municipalities to meet.

The heavy reliance on RVAs should not, however, overshadow the consequences of a risk management based logic that can depoliticise public policies on climate change by embedding security—and by extension, adaptation—within technocratic routines that prioritise management over political contestation or ethical debate. As we have pointed out in Chap. 2, Security Studies scholars have increasingly adopted the language and logic of risk, influenced by scholars like Beck and Foucault. This shift reflects a move from threat deterrence to risk prevention, resilience, and long-term governance.

This insight is critical in the context of flood risk governance, where policies that appear technically sound (e.g. zoning rules, early warning systems) may obscure deeper political questions about whose risks are prioritised, who pays, and whose knowledge counts. The 2023 storm Hans is a case in point: despite prior data and modelling, the consequences revealed the limits of technocratic planning and the systemic weaknesses in coordination, legitimacy, and understanding of residual risk. Even with sophisticated flood mapping and regulation, residual risk—the risk that remains when all reasonable preventive measures have been taken—cannot be eliminated. Managing this demands a preparedness capacity that is forward-looking and flexible, not merely reactive. Thus, bowtie diagrams and other traditional risk models are useful but insufficient for dealing with deep uncertainty and societal complexity, such as cascading effects across infrastructures or disproportionate impacts on vulnerable groups.

Thus, flood risk is emblematic of the broader dilemmas in climate change adaptation governance: how to govern under uncertainty and residual risk, coordinate across administrative and sectoral boundaries, balance prevention with preparedness, and ensure legitimacy in the face of rising expectations and growing risks. Integrating insights from Security Studies and Risk Governance disciplines allows us to see flood risk not just as a physical or administrative challenge, but as a governance problem shaped by knowledge, power, and contested futures.

References

Aaheim, A. (Ed.). (2009). *Konsekvenser av klimaendringer, tilpasning og sårbarhet i Norge: Rapport til Klimatilpasningsutvalget*. Cicero Senter for klimaforskning.

Alfieri, L., Burek, P.-A., Feyen, L., & Forzieri, G. (2015). Global warming increases the frequency of river floods in Europe. *Hydrology and Earth System Sciences, 19*(5), 2247–2260. https://doi.org/10.5194/hess-19-2247-2015

Alfieri, L., Feyen, L., & Di Baldassarre, G. (2016). Increasing flood risk under climate change: A pan-European assessment of the benefits of four adaptation strategies. *Climatic Change, 136*, 507–521. https://doi.org/10.1007/s10584-016-1641-1

De Ruijter, A., & Guldenmund, F. (2016). The bowtie method: A review. *Safety Science, 88*, 211–218. https://doi.org/10.1016/j.ssci.2016.03.001

DSB. (2022). *Veileder til helhetlig risiko- og sårbarhetsanalyse i kommunen En metodeveileder for helhetlig ROS i kommunal beredskapsplikt*. Direktoratet for samfunnssikkerhet og beredskap (DSB).

DSB. (2024). *Evaluering av ekstremværet Hans – forebygging, beredskap og håndtering*. Direktoratet for samfunnssikkerhet og beredskap (DSB).

Hanssen-Bauer, I., Førland, E. J., Haddeland, I., Hisdal, H., Mayer, S., Nesje, A., Nilsen, J., Even, Ø., Sandven, S., Sandø, A. B., Sorteberg, A., & og Ådlandsvik, B. (Eds.). (2016). *Klima i Norge 2100: Kunnskapsgrunnlag for klimatilpasning oppdatert i 2015*. Norsk klimaservicesenter.

IPCC Intergovernmental Panel on Climate Change. (2023). *Climate change 2022: Impacts, adaptation and vulnerability*. Contribution of Working Group II to the Sixth Assessment Report of the Intergovernmental Panel on Climate Change [H.-O. Pörtner, D. C. Roberts, M. Tignor, E. S. Poloczanska, K. Mintenbeck, A. Alegría, M. Craig, S. Langsdorf, S. Löschke, V. Möller, A. Okem, & B. Rama (Eds.)]. Cambridge University Press. https://doi.org/10.1017/9781009325844

Karlson, C. W., Morsut, C., & Engen, O. A. (2023). Politics of climate risk management in local government: A case study of the municipality of Stavanger. *Frontiers in Climate, 5*, 1136673.

Kruke, B. I. (2012). *Societal safety and crisis management: Relevance for 22 July 2011*. 22 July-Commission Paper.

Meld. St. 15 (2011–2012). (2012). *Hvordan leve med farene – om flom og skred*. Olje- og energidepartementet.

Meld. St. 26 (2022–2023). (2023). *Report to the storting (white paper) A changing climate – United for a climate-resilient society*. Norwegian Ministry of Climate and Environment. English version.

Meld. St. 27 (2023–2024). (2024). *Tryggare framtid – førebudd på flaum og skred*. Energidepartementet. https://www.regjeringen.no/contentassets/7a6bf454917444a18225bd8cdebfbff3/nn-no/pdfs/stm202320240027000dddpdfs.pdf

MET. (2023). *The extreme weather Hans is bringing an extremely large amount of rain over Southern Norway*. Accessed June 18, 2025, from https://www.met.no/en/archive/the-extreme-weather-hans-is-bringing-an-extremely-large-amount-of-rain-over-southern-norway

Morsut, C., Engen, O. A., Neby, S., & Angell, E. (2024). Translations of climate change consequences at the local level: Climate change adaptation in Bergen and Stavanger municipalities in Norway. *Risk, Hazards & Crisis in Public Policy, 15*(4), 468–490.

Neby, S. (2019). Climate adaptation and preparedness in Norway: Third order effects, small-scale wickedness and governance capacity. *International Public Management Review, 19*(2), 26–46.

Neby, S., Angell, E., Engen, O. A., & Morsut, C. (2023a). Klimatilpasning i Norge: Mellom risiko, beredskap og normalsituasjon. *Norsk statsvitenskapelig tidsskrift, 39*(4), 159–176.

Neby, S., Engen, O. A., Morsut, C., & Angell, E. (2023b). Klimakrisen, klimarisiko og innrammingen av norsk klimapolitikk. *Stat og Styring, 33*(2), 16–21. https://doi.org/10.18261/stat.33.2.4

Norsk klimaservicesenter. (2025). *Klimaprofilene – et kunnskapsgrunnlag for klimatilpasning*. Accessed June 13, 2025, from https://klimaservicesenter.no/kss/klimaprofiler/om

NOU 2018: 17. (2018). *Klimarisiko og norsk økonomi*. Finansdepartementet. https://www.regjeringen.no/contentassets/c5119502a03145278c33b72d9060fbc9/no/pdfs/nou201820180017000dddpdfs.pdf

NOU 2023: 17. (2023). *Nå er det alvor – Rustet for en usikker fremtid*. Justis- og beredskapsdepartementet. https://www.regjeringen.no/contentassets/4b9ba57bebae44d2bebfc845ff6cd5f5/no/pdfs/nou202320230017000dddpdfs.pdf

Plan- og bygningsloven. (2008). *Lov 27. juni 2008 nr. 71 om planlegging og byggesaksbehandling*. Accessed June 18, 2025, from https://lovdata.no/dokument/NL/lov/2008-06-27-71

Regulation. (2018). *Forskrift 28. september 2018 nr. 1469 Statlige planretningslinjer for klima- og energiplanlegging og klimatilpasning*. Accessed June 18, 2025, from https://lovdata.no/dokument/LTI/forskrift/2018-09-28-1469

Renn, O. (2008). *Risk governance: Coping with uncertainty in a complex world.* Routledge.

Riksrevisjonen. (2025). *Riksrevisjonens undersøkelse av myndighetenes arbeid med å tilpasse infrastruktur og bebyggelse til et klima i endring.* Accessed June 18, 2025, from https://www.stortinget.no/no/Saker-og-publikasjoner/Saker/Sak/?p=88313

Sivilbeskyttelsesloven. (2010). *Lov 25. juni 2010 nr. 45 om kommunal beredskapsplikt, sivile beskyttelsestiltak og Sivilforsvaret.* Accessed June 18, 2025, from https://lovdata.no/dokument/NL/lov/2010-06-25-45

Taleb, N. (2010). The Black Swan: The Impact of the Highly Improbable, 2nd ed.. Random House.

TEK 17. (2025). *Byggteknisk forskrift (TEK17) med veiledning.* Accessed June 18, 2025, from https://www.dibk.no/regelverk/byggteknisk-forskrift-tek17

UNDRR United Nations Office for Disaster Risk Reduction. (2017a). The Sendai framework terminology on disaster risk reduction. *Residual risk.* Accessed June 18, 2025, from https://www.undrr.org/terminology/residual-risk

UNDRR United Nations Office for Disaster Risk Reduction. (2017b). The Sendai framework terminology on disaster risk reduction. *Resilience.* Accessed June 18, 2025, from https://www.undrr.org/terminology/resilience

UNDRR United Nations Office for Disaster Risk Reduction. (2017c). The Sendai framework terminology on disaster risk reduction. *Prevention.* Accessed June 18, 2025, from https://www.undrr.org/terminology/prevention

UNDRR United Nations Office for Disaster Risk Reduction. (2017d). The Sendai framework terminology on disaster risk reduction. *Preparedness.* Accessed June 18, 2025, from https://www.undrr.org/terminology/preparedness

CHAPTER 7

Implications of a Risk Management Approach Within Climate Change Adaptation for Research and Practice

Claudia Morsut, Mark Rhinard, and Ole Andreas Engen

Abstract This final chapter brings together the central themes explored throughout the contributions to the book, which examined the growing prominence of risk management in climate change adaptation governance. While adaptation is now widely recognised as essential for managing the impacts of climate change, the ways in which it is governed remain contested. This book focused on the implications of treating adaptation primarily as a matter of risk management—both in theory and in practice. It asked: *What are the consequences, both intended and unintended, of governing adaptation through a logic of risk?* Is risk management a comprehensive approach to adaptation or does it encourage only incremental changes? In answering this question, the chapters have engaged with debates in Security Studies and Risk Governance, analysed developments at the

C. Morsut (✉) • O. A. Engen
University of Stavanger, Stavanger, Norway
e-mail: claudia.morsut@uis.no; ole.a.engen@uis.no

M. Rhinard
Stockholm University, Stockholm, Sweden
e-mail: mark.rhinard@ekohist.su.se

C. Morsut (ed.), *Adapting to Climate Change*,
https://doi.org/10.1007/978-3-032-07136-1_7

international, national, and local levels, and explored how adaptation unfolds through institutions, models, and discourses. This chapter reflects on the key theoretical insights, synthesises the empirical patterns, discusses implications for policy and governance, and outlines promising directions for future research.

Keywords Climate change adaptation • Governance • Risk management

7.1 Introduction

This book started in Chap. 1 by describing the severe impacts climate change poses to our societies and the two main streams of literature of reference. The literature from Security Studies, through securitisation theory, posits that climate change is a threat that requires an urgent and compelling response, while Risk Governance scholars address climate change impacts in terms of climate risks or systemic risks and propose risk-based approaches, like risk management, as the main way to cope with a changing climate. Then, the book outlined the relevance of climate change adaptation, as one of the two responses international organisations and states use to cope with climate change impacts, by offering, in the central chapters, a series of reflections on what a risk management approach means for climate change adaptation. While Chap. 2 clarified the understanding of risk in the two literatures of reference, calling for a genuine interdisciplinary effort, Chap. 3 deepened the issues of systemic risks governance in dealing with adaptation. Chapter 4 took stock of the development of risk management models in international climate change adaptation governance. The chapter argued that despite the incorporation of a larger amount of data to analyse climate risks, these models, investing in the adaptation of a technocratic stance, have yet to overcome issues related to climate justice. Chapter 5 introduced the issue of legitimation in understanding Norwegian adaptation governance. Risk management in Norway has a central role in framing adaptation policies. However, at the same time, it is intertwined with other approaches, such as municipal planning and societal safety and security. Chapter 6 considered the management of flood risk at the local level in Norway and the effects it has on adaptation, examining the interplay between prevention and preparedness.

7.2 Implications of Risk Management Approaches in Theory and Practice

The main question we raised at the beginning of the book concerned the theoretical and empirical implications of using risk management in climate change adaptation. As the chapters explored, climate change adaptation has become increasingly shaped by a risk management logic. This section reflects on the implications of that shift. We ask whether risk management offers a comprehensive and transformative framework for adaptation, or whether it reinforces incremental, expert-driven routines that narrow the field of political and practical possibilities. Drawing from the dual theoretical anchor points of Security Studies and Risk Governance, we consider how risk-based adaptation reshapes core concepts such as risk, uncertainty, legitimacy, and responsibility and influences governance and policy-making in the face of complex climate change challenges. We also examine how these dynamics play out in practice, influencing how adaptation is institutionalised across governance levels and policy sectors. This section first looks at implications for theory before turning to implications for practice.

7.2.1 *Theoretical Implications*

Climate change adaptation has increasingly been approached through the lens of risk, and this book has drawn primarily on two literatures to interrogate that shift: Security Studies and Risk Governance. Security Studies scholars have explored how the rise of risk-based thinking has reshaped security practices, influencing how threats are constructed, managed, and governed. Risk Governance offers a more procedural and technocratic account of how uncertainty can be managed through anticipatory tools and participatory mechanisms. These literatures stem from different epistemological traditions—Security Studies often grounded in critical and constructivist approaches, Risk Governance in systems thinking and institutional design—but they converge in their concern with how societies respond to uncertain, disruptive futures. It tends to question whether the assumptions of preparedness and institutional responsiveness embedded in risk frameworks hold up under real-world conditions, especially during fast-moving or cascading crises. This tension—between the logic of control and the reality of turbulence—runs through the analysis of risk-based adaptation in this book.

One theoretical implication of our research is to show that through the application of risk management thinking, risk itself has become a *governing technology*. The expansive use of risk models and risk and vulnerability analyses does more than describe the world; it shapes it. As shown through Chaps. 2–6, such approaches help define which problems are seen as urgent, which actors are empowered to act, and which types of knowledge count. Theorists should pay closer attention to how risk modelling and risk analysis operate as a form of power that structures agendas and institutional authority. Risk models and analyses contribute, as well, to depoliticising adaptation, which is framed as a technical and managerial issue. The risk is that adaptation is not a pressing issue to pursue, but one of the several measures watered down in a plethora of prevention and preparedness solutions, as Chaps. 5 and 6 point out. While this can streamline action, it also narrows the scope for democratic debate and suppresses value-based disagreements, and overshadows power dynamics and political choices.

Theoretical work should explore how such depoliticisation affects the legitimacy and diversity of adaptation pathways. Legitimacy, together with responsibility in multi-level governance, is an issue that has been challenged especially in Chap. 5, which points out how risk governance spreads across scales, but often without clarity about who is responsible for what in the case of adaptation. This fragmentation can obscure accountability and weaken legitimacy. Theorists should examine how authority and responsibility are constructed—and often blurred—within polycentric governance systems. All the chapters in this book have made references to the relevance of governing uncertainty as the primary goal of risk management through the incorporation of tools such as probabilistic reasoning, foresight, and scenario planning. This can enable anticipatory governance, but may also oversimplify complex risks, induce residual risk, and, in general, create a misleading sense of control.

Even more concerning, anticipatory governance can *normalise* uncertainty, as inherent to climate change impacts and climate risks. This uncertainty becomes something that can be managed and governed solely through risk management tools. As such, adaptation moves away from deterministic planning towards probabilistic reasoning, scenario analysis, and precautionary principles. As Beck reminds us, it is not possible to achieve a completely risk-free society, nor is it desirable. Scholars of risk management would be wise to consider how uncertainty is made 'actionable', to what extent uncertainty should be avoided and at what cost, and which trade-offs exist in accepting a risk society.

Finally, while risk management relies heavily on expert-led risk assessments, it can overlook local knowledge and marginalise public participation. As shown in the Norwegian empirical cases, this creates tensions between centralised expertise and place-based needs. Norway is an example of a country where adaptation governance seems caught in the middle between technocratic rationality promoted by national authorities and local knowledge. Theory should consider the relationship between formal expertise and locally grounded, participatory approaches to adaptation and how the two interact. Technocratic rationality can be useful at first but needs to meet deliberative governance that emphasises inclusion, equity, and legitimacy since adaptation measures unfold locally and need to be contextualised.

7.2.2 *Implications for Practice*

While the theoretical implications of risk-based adaptation governance help illuminate how power, knowledge, and legitimacy are structured, it is equally important to examine how these dynamics unfold in practice. After all, risk management approaches do not remain confined to discourse or as an abstract model. They shape concrete policies, institutions, administrative routines, and even societal norms. In the context of climate change adaptation, risk management influences how policies are designed, implemented, and evaluated. It introduces structured decision-making through tools such as risk and vulnerability assessments, cost-benefit analyses, scenario planning, and early warning systems, all of which aim to govern uncertainty.

These tools enable the prioritisation of adaptation measures. For example, cost-benefit analyses help determine where to allocate resources, while early warning systems improve preparedness and reduce disaster response costs. A key strength of risk management lies in its data-driven nature, drawing on empirical data to support evidence-based policy. However, this technocratic orientation can reduce adaptation to a set of administrative routines, limiting the potential for more transformative change.

Moreover, countries differ in their capacity to manage climate risks. Those with more robust administrative and technical capabilities are better positioned to carry out risk assessments and implement adaptation measures. Without explicit attention to equity, risk management may inadvertently reinforce existing inequalities between countries. As Chap. 4 concludes, institutions such as the United Nations and the European Union have an important role to play in providing risk management models to their member states. These models must be coupled with inclusive governance approaches that promote just adaptation, such as the integration of data on inequalities and socio-economic vulnerabilities.

For national and local officials, our findings carry important implications. At the national level, officials would be wise to balance technical precision with political legitimacy, ensuring that risk assessments do not become detached from public values or democratic processes. They face the task of integrating complex models into national planning systems while also adapting them to domestic institutional and socio-economic contexts. For local officials, the context may be different, but the stakes are no less pressing. Often on the frontline of climate impacts, they must operationalise risk-based models in ways that reflect local vulnerabilities, community priorities, and available resources. Yet these actors frequently lack the technical tools, resources, or decision authority to influence upstream modelling processes that lead to top-down requirements. This disconnect suggests the need for capacity-building efforts that not only transfer knowledge but also empower local actors to shape how risk is defined, prioritised, and governed in an era of complex adaptation needs.

7.3 Looking Back and Looking Ahead

To conclude, this book has explored a central dilemma in contemporary adaptation governance: Does risk management enable the kind of transformative change required to address the climate crisis, or does it instead reinforce incrementalism and system stability? By analysing the nature of risk-based policy-making, we questioned whether this approach can fully respond to the complex, contested, and multi-scalar challenges posed by climate change.

Through the RISKSEC2.0 project, we learned how valuable the study of adaptation is not only in a multi-governance level, but also in a cross-country comparative fashion. We call for more research on adaptation that relies on case studies to compare. Especially at the local level, comparative studies show variation in adaptation practices, the use of local knowledge in context-specific governance settings, and openness for discussions on lessons learned and possible replicability of adaptation measures. We encourage research about epistemic communities and power to investigate how expert networks shape the diffusion and institutionalisation of risk models across governance levels, as highlighted in Chaps. 4 and 5. More research is also needed on the relationship between legitimacy and adaptation, which remains under-examined in multi-level governance settings. Greater attention should also be directed towards the role of civil society, including citizen participation and perceptions, in adaptation governance, particularly in contexts where strong epistemic communities, often expert-led and risk-based, shape adaptation policies and practices. Finally, we propose studies which shed light on how risk models prioritise what can be measured, potentially sidelining deeper concerns like justice, vulnerability, and political accountability. The key question to address here is whether institutions govern risks that are framed through models, and are assessed and analysed by existing risk management tools or should rather deal with the most urgent or socially salient, like inequality.

Indeed, risk management offers anticipatory capacity and procedural clarity, and it has become the dominant approach of adaptation governance across scales. However, by normalising uncertainty and privileging technical expertise, it often marginalises political contestation, downplays structural inequality, and risks excluding local knowledge. As shown in Chaps. 3–5, expert-driven models help govern uncertainty but can obscure power relations and legitimate only certain forms of knowledge. In Norway, adaptation is closely entwined with planning laws and societal safety and security discourses, reinforcing a technocratic logic that shapes not only how adaptation is implemented, but also who is responsible and what action counts as legitimate.

While risk management operates from global frameworks down to local practices, it raises important questions about coordination, equity, and legitimacy. Well-resourced actors are often best positioned to benefit from risk-based governance, while vulnerable communities may remain underrepresented unless justice and inclusion are made explicit priorities. A just adaptation requires more than data and foresight—it demands participatory processes and normative reflection on whose futures are being protected.

One of this book's key contributions lies in bringing together insights from Security Studies and Risk Governance to show how risk-based adaptation both enables and constrains. Adaptation is not only a matter of managing impacts—it is a process of negotiating values, allocating responsibility, and shaping collective futures in conditions of uncertainty. The tools of risk management remain valuable, but they must be embedded within governance approaches that are inclusive, critical, and socially aware. Without attention to justice, participation, and legitimacy, even the most sophisticated models will fall short. Effective adaptation is not only about managing risk—it is about transforming governance.

Index[1]

[1] Note: Page numbers followed by 'n' refer to notes.

C. Morsut (ed.), *Adapting to Climate Change*,
https://doi.org/10.1007/978-3-032-07136-1

Kolibri 360 GmbH
Ferdinand-Jühlke-Straße 7
99095 Erfurt, Deutschland
produktsicherheit@kolibri360.de